A Social Science Student's Guide to Surviving Your PhD

A Social Science Student's Guide to Surviving Your PhD

Kohol Shadrach Iornem, PhD

 Open University Press

Open University Press
McGraw Hill
8th Floor, 338 Euston Road
London
England
NW1 3BH

email: enquiries@openup.co.uk
world wide web: www.openup.co.uk

and Two Penn Plaza, New York, NY 10121-2289, USA

First edition published 2021

A catalogue record of this book is available from the British Library

ISBN-13: 9780335249633
ISBN-10: 0335249639
eISBN: 9780335249640

Library of Congress Cataloging-in-Publication Data
CIP data applied for

Typeset by Transforma Pvt. Ltd., Chennai, India

Praise page

This book is written by a successful survivor! This clear and supportive text provides a detailed synthesis of, and rationale for, the key issues involved in a PhD and is highly recommended for anyone contemplating embarking on a PhD programme - it should be read from start to finish before starting the journey and consulted at regular intervals throughout the journey using the lists of dos and don'ts as checklists at strategic milestones along the way.

Professor Eleri Jones, Professor Emerita,
Cardiff Metropolitan University

Dr Iornem presents the topic of a PhD journey in the same way as he undertook the journey itself: with enthusiasm and joy. Any student wanting to tackle this daunting task should use this book as a guide and as a motivator. Dr Iornem recognizes the hurdles and the fears which face a research student and addresses them with realism, pragmatism and humour, based on his own personal experiences.

Dr John Koenigsberger (PhD supervisor: Cardiff Metropolitan
University; University of Wales, Trinity St. Davids)

From development of the research proposal to preparing for the viva voce and post-doctoral career options, this handy survival guide provides an invaluable source of advice and inside knowledge on the entire PhD process. All stages are explained in simple terms, and potential pitfalls are clearly highlighted, along with how to avoid them. This accessible, informative and engaging book is highly recommended as essential reading to anyone considering undertaking a PhD.

Dr Hillary J. Shaw, Senior Research Fellow, Centre for
Urban Research on Austerity, De Montfort University

My first meeting with Kohol was on the MBA programme when he was an international student. After successfully completing the MBA programme he enrolled for the PhD programme as he wanted to pursue an academic career. The PhD journey is a lonely journey. This book is a very good reflection and personal experience on Dr Kohol's journey as an international student on the PhD programme. He has explained the process from the start to finish and this book is a must read for all the prospective international students who wish to enrol for a doctoral programme. I am confident that this book will be a source of inspiration for many students.

Dr Rajendra Kumar, FCMI, FCIM, SFHEA, MBA Programme Leader,
London School of Commerce, DBA Director of Studies at the University
of the West of Scotland and the University of Wales Trinity Saint

I dedicate this book to two unique Tiv sons – the late Apollos Aper
Aku and the late Ezekiel Aker Akiga, who were the first
university graduates from Tivland.

Aper Aku was the first civilian governor of Benue State, Nigeria.
His praiseworthy contributions to education, capacity building
and the developmental foundation he established in
Benue are everlasting and iconic tributes to a gentleman
who was head and shoulders above the rest – a true patriot.

Aker Akiga was appointed Head of Service by Aper Aku.
Like his mentor, he pioneered numerous contributions to education.

Table of contents

List of figures   xii

List of tables   xiii

About the author   xiv

Foreword   xv

Preface   xvii

Acknowledgements   xx

1   THE UPS AND DOWNS OF A SUCCESSFUL PHD JOURNEY   1

    Overview   1
    Examples of the questions   2
    International students' experiences   3
    Themes from interview questions   8
    Conclusions and recommendations from the interviews   10
    Areas of further research   11
    Chapter 1: summary   11

2   CONCERNS, RESERVATIONS AND FEARS ABOUT STARTING A PHD   12

    Introduction   12
    Suggestions   14
    Chapter 2: summary   14

3   THE PHD JOURNEY IN SUMMARY – FROM START TO FINISH   15

    Funding   15
    The application and entry requirements   17
    Research proposal writing   17
    Contacting potential supervisors   19
    The interview   20
    Upgrade or transfer to a PhD   20
    Annual monitoring report (AMR)   20
    Mock viva   21
    Viva voce   21
    Chapter 3: summary   22

4	WHAT IS A PHD?	23
	Thesis or dissertation?	23
	Original research explained	24
	Four possible ways to develop originality	24
	Extensive research	26
	Planning your research	29
	Chapter 4: summary	31
5	RESEARCH SKILLS REQUIRED	32
	Plagiarism – the assassin that terrorizes the world of academia	32
	Ensuring consistency in referencing	37
	Dealing with Time Thieves – suggested success tips	38
	Top eight Time Thieves to avoid	38
	Join a Research Interest Group	43
	Presenting your research using PowerPoint	44
	Chapter 5: summary	46
6	STRUCTURE OF A GOOD PHD THESIS	47
	PhD thesis word count – a guide	47
	Thesis structure	47
	Word count for each chapter	48
	Thesis argumentation	49
	Writing an abstract	51
	Chapter 6: summary	52
7	DOING A PHD: WHY IT IS IMPORTANT TO PUBLISH	53
	Publishing your research	53
	The importance of publishing	54
	Adapting to each publication's requirements	55
	Considering career options: academia or other employment?	55
	Chapter 7: summary	57
8	HOW TO KEEP YOURSELF MOTIVATED	58
	Introduction	58
	My supervisory team	59
	My dad	60
	My proofreader	60
	My colleague	60
	My PhD friends at other universities	61
	My family	61
	My professional capacity	62
	Chapter 8: summary	62

9   PROOFREADING AND EDITING   63

    Find a professional proofreader   63
    Chapter 9: summary   65

10 HANDLING CHANGES RECOMMENDED BY SUPERVISORS   66
    AND EXAMINERS

    Supervisors and examiners want you to pass, but . . .   66
    Saving time on corrections   67
    Dealing with amendments – my story   68
    Chapter 10: summary   69

11 MOCK VIVA AND VIVA VOCE PREPARATION   70

    Appointing an external examiner   70
    Make it easy for the examiner to read your hard work   71
    What examiners look out for in a thesis   73
    Facing difficult examiners   77
    Dos and don'ts of a successful viva   78
    Online viva and meetings   82
    Chapter 11: summary   83

12 THE VIVA EXPERIENCE   84

    My viva experience – typical of what happens   84
    Sample viva questions   89
    Chapter 12: summary   91

Appendices   92

Appendix A   A guide to summarizing your thesis   93

Appendix B   Summarizing literature sources   95

References   101

Index   105

List of figures

Figure 1   Thesis or dissertation   23
Figure 2   PhD – an extension of the body of knowledge   26
Figure 3   Preferred   45
Figure 4   Avoid (too much text)   45
Figure 5   Readable   46
Figure 6   Avoid (unreadable – text blends with background)   46
Figure 7   3S approach to thesis writing   49
Figure 8   Writing up your thesis   50

List of tables

Table 1 My research summary for the viva voce examination   93
Table 2 Key authors that influenced my study on Nigerian universities   95
         (country-specific literature sources)
Table 3 Other key authors that influenced my study   98
Table 4 New research development after thesis submission   100
         (before the viva)

About the author

Kohol Shadrach Iornem, PhD, is a senior lecturer at the International Foundation Group, where he teaches Business Management, Research Methods and Study Skills to students enrolled on the Pre-PhD Preparation Programme. He is also the Director of Programmes at the London Graduate School. In this position, he provides guidance, advice and facilitation in all aspects of organizational development, from strategy formulation to change management.

Kohol is the author of 'Job satisfaction and turnover intentions among university lecturers in Nigeria' (PhD thesis). He has published articles in peer-reviewed journals, presented papers at academic conferences, and also chaired conference sessions for the Human Resource Management track and Organizational Transformation, Change and Development track at the British Academy of Management. Kohol holds a PhD in Management from Cardiff Metropolitan University, an MBA from the University of Wales Institute, Cardiff, and a Bachelor of Engineering in Metallurgical Engineering from the Ahmadu Bello University, Nigeria.

In his tenure as President of the Mutual Union of Tiv in the United Kingdom (MUTUK) – a registered charity – Kohol has gained proven leadership experience. He enjoys promoting and enhancing the socio-economic and cultural development of Tiv people in the UK and supporting similar advancements in Tivland, Nigeria.

Foreword

Studying for a PhD is the most lonely, frustrating, masochistic and ultimately incredibly rewarding project a student can embark on. You're going to need your friends to help you and, based on Hemingway's comment that 'There is no friend as loyal as a book', *A Social Science Student's Guide to Surviving your PhD* is an invaluable companion throughout your journey (Hemingway, n.d.). There are plenty of worthy and informative books, articles and university web-sites available with good advice for PhD students; but this book, written by someone who has recently completed his PhD, is more informal and approachable. Good friends are there for you, whenever you need them, to give you helpful and practical suggestions, to put an arm round you when you're frustrated and discouraged, to give you a kick up the backside when your self-pity is taking over, and to celebrate with you when things are going well. This book meets all those needs and more.

Perhaps the best quality of this book is the immediacy of someone who has only just completed his doctoral journey. I have known Kohol since he came to our college from Nigeria some ten years ago, and have stayed in touch with him ever since as he completed his MBA and then progressed onto his PhD studies. Like many students, he has had to balance his studies with the demands of a young family and the need to develop his own business interests. He has had to be self-disciplined and resolute, and the overall message of the book is 'If I can do it, then so can you'.

In a subjective, informal and practical way, he has covered all the hurdles that PhD students need to deal with. Not least of these is the initial decision on the research topic. I have lost count of the number of prospective PhD students who have told me they want to do a PhD on marketing or on cyber security, etc without having any real idea of the specific field. The section of this book describing how Kohol developed his ideas is particularly useful, finding a topic which was relevant to his previous postgraduate studies, could be researched using relatively accessible sources, and which made a valid contribution to the academic literature in his field.

The whole application process for a PhD is almost as exhausting as the degree which follows as you have to find a university which will accept you, find a supervisor at that university who is willing and able to take you on, find the finance you require and develop the patience you need waiting for replies from academics whose idea of a quick response is often – well, not very quick at all.

Kohol then summarizes, in a fresh and easily understood way, the many different research skills students need to acquire – from avoiding plagiarism to literature reviews, methodology, publishing, and so on. You should take note especially of his advice to students as they approach the dreaded final viva.

A Social Science Student's Guide to Surviving your PhD is a particularly invaluable companion for international students whose previous studies in their own country have not really prepared them for PhD studies elsewhere. At our college we teach many such students on our Pre-PhD course and are lucky to have Kohol as one of our tutors on this. I will be advising all our students to keep a copy of his book on their bedside tables and I reckon that it will be very well-worn by the time they finish their studies.

This book meets a genuine need which will be appreciated by all research students, wherever they come from. It's concise, compact and practical. In the course of your studies, you'll buy many longer and much more expensive books, but I reckon this one may well be your best investment.

Michael Addison
Academic Director
International Foundation Group
September 2020

Preface

The inspiration for writing this book found its beginnings at the height of my academic achievement, my PhD graduation in 2017, during which Professor Cara Carmichael Aitchison offered the following words of encouragement:

> Congratulations! We are proud of you. Wherever you go in the world, there will always be someone admiring you, wanting to be like you, because you are a role model. And we would ask, just occasionally, that you turn to the person standing behind you and give them a helping hand. Because there are many people, I am sure, who have reached out to you with a helping hand, offered a word of encouragement or opened doors.

After earning my doctorate, I began teaching research and study skills to post-graduate students seeking to enrol on a PhD programme. As my career advanced, so did my awareness of a common theme among a number of my Pre-PhD students: a difficulty in choosing an appropriate research topic or area. Some frequently ask why it takes many years to complete the programme, when a great many people are, seemingly, unable to do so within a stipulated study period. Others, by comparison, are usually concerned with the quality of their work and whether it will meet the standards expected of a PhD.

In my attempt to address the subject, I began by compiling all the relevant academic notes I had ever taken, starting from the beginning of my PhD journey in 2013 and leading up to the present day. The idea was to collate them into perspectives for this book, thus taking those first steps to truly embrace my professor's advice – i.e. looking back and giving a helping hand. The aim was to guide current and prospective students in overcoming some of the study challenges which I and numerous other students have experienced.

As is the case with any project one embarks on for the first time, challenges are aplenty. Well, this is my very own story aboard the PhD journey! On many occasions, while attempting to address some of my research-related problems, I struggled to find useful resources both on the internet and in print. One such example remains vivid, taking me back to when I was not sure about the chapter word count requirements in my written research. I had to rely on the university library's dissertation samples to get an idea of the guideline specifications. Well, it seems I neither was nor remain alone in that struggle. To this day, many doctoral students seek my advice when it comes to defining the word count specification for their research chapters.

You may be wondering what qualifies me to write this book. First and foremost, I am proud to say that I was the only student in my cohort to complete the PhD programme within the expected four-year period, back in 2017. It was no small feat as, after me, the next student in my group to graduate did so as late as March 2020. This leads me to believe that I must have navigated through my

PhD journey using study techniques that proved advantageous and helped me 'reach the finish line' within the stipulated time frame. It is for this reason that I now share the success of my academic journey and knowledge so that others could emulate.

Secondly, as an academic teaching Research Methods and Study Skills, I can offer valuable field-specific guidance to aspiring students. I currently supervise two PhD students. The in-depth knowledge of my specialism is rewarded by the success of one of my students who has already completed her thesis and graduated. In addition to these examples of my professional profile, I have, through ambition and dedication, recently published my PhD thesis, 'Job satisfaction and turnover intentions among university lecturers in Nigeria', published articles in peer-reviewed journals as well as presented papers at academic conferences (Iornem, 2017, 2018, 2020a). In the past, I have chaired conferences, most notably a session at the Human Resource Management track and the Organizational Transformation, and Change and Development event at the British Academy of Management Conference.

What makes this book unique is that it gives a true account of my personal experience as a PhD student, how I faced and managed obstacles on my study path, and what solutions I am now in a position to offer to students facing similar challenges. Each chapter of the book is equally important. However, I believe you will particularly benefit from drawing valuable conclusions from the ups and downs of other PhD students' journeys that I have shared on these pages. As someone who has completed the programme in a timely manner, I can provide insightful knowledge about the reasons for the choices I had made during my own doctorate studies and, in particular, how dilemmas that inevitably occurred were resolved.

I have given a snapshot of what you can expect on the PhD journey, from start to finish. I have also highlighted the essential research skills you require to complete your studies successfully. This includes advice on avoiding plagiarism, managing your time on the journey, and taking into consideration your study–family–work balance. I have also explained the benefit of joining Research Interest Groups as a PhD student.

A PhD, some say, is an original contribution to knowledge. How do you ensure your work is original? In essence, Chapter 4 explains this aptly. In addition to originality, maintaining your peak energy levels is also an important element of the PhD journey. With that in mind, I have included a chapter on motivation, which portrays my story and the sources from which I derived my own guidance.

On your academic journey, you may temporarily lose contact with a lot of people. The one person likely to be with you throughout your studies, however, is your supervisor. Therefore, I have offered advice on how to maintain a trusting and inspirational student–supervisor relationship, and how to approach criticism from your supervisory team positively and proactively, so as to achieve your desired academic result.

They say everything that has a beginning must have an end. So a point will come when you reach the finish line – your final viva. For this reason, I have dedicated two entire chapters to academic suggestions to prepare you for it. This includes a variety of frequently asked sample questions, which you can practise with your peers or family members before your oral exam.

This book is relevant to doctoral/PhD students in social sciences, and their supervisors. Students will relate well to it on both academic and emotional levels, as the doctorate is quite an emotional undertaking. The use of a variety of examples from different cultures, combined with my experience of studying in the UK as an overseas student, will be particularly useful to international students who may not be fully informed of the application process and demands of research degrees in the UK or other Anglophile countries.

As already mentioned, I have personally experienced and benefitted from undertaking the PhD journey. I believe this is a heartfelt story – one which will be very appealing as well as informative to anyone preparing for, or already committed to, research writing. For this reason, I have structured the book as an informal, light and comprehensive guide. Its strength lies in the approachable and conversational style I have adopted, and the messages, which I have kept simple.

Acknowledgements

Although this book is based on my research experience, many people have offered help, advice and encouragement in one way or the other. While it is not possible to mention every person, I would like to express my sincere appreciation to some of those who offered valued input.

I give God the glory for the knowledge I have acquired and which I can now share with other academics.

I would like to thank my friend and mentor, Professor Bruce Duncan, who worked through sleepless nights and long days proofreading and editing my book on a pro bono basis. His contribution is priceless. Professor Michael Addison, my friend and mentor, provided opportunities for me to teach the Pre-PhD students at the International Foundation Group in London. The probing questions from these students necessitated the completion of this book.

For the development and production of the book, I feel a deep sense of gratitude to Beth Summers and Sam Crowe at Open University Press for their feedback, support and editorial suggestions. Dr Cynthia Ndeh inspired me on my PhD journey, and many of the milestones successfully passed bear her name. Thank you, Dr Ndeh. I am also indebted to the senior academics Lillian Dekic, Dr Andrea Charles Fidelis, Dr Teslim Bukoye, Dr John Koenigsberger and Dr Hillary Shaw. Their guidance, constructive comments and indispensable mentorship helped me walk the long road to success.

Special appreciation to my friends at the Christ Royal Assembly and MUTUK. These amazing people not only motivated and inspired me but carried me in their prayers. I would like to thank those who provided encouragement and helpful comments in the final stages of the book, especially Kevin Korgba, Vivian Kave, Adukwu Sule, Chigozie Nwarize, Aondoakaa Fele, David Atama, Sophia Kwaghzan, Pamela Okochi, Bem Agera and Dr Stephen Akuma.

On a more personal note, let me turn to Prof David Iornem, my beloved father, who set me on my journey. His encouragement and exemplar leadership have brought me to this part of my odyssey. His mentorship paved the way for me. Then, too, my mums, Esther and Member, and brothers and sisters – Shima, Doomama, Hangem, Fanen, Fanyam, Ana and Nabem – always stood by me.

Last, but by no means least, I must acknowledge my gratitude and appreciation to my beautiful and patient wife, Sadiksha, who kept everything going while I drafted the manuscript, not only feeding me constantly but also sharing ideas leading to the completion of this book – and to our two adorable daughters, Jemima and Samantha, for without them, I would have completed this book much earlier!

1 The ups and downs of a successful PhD journey

By the end of this chapter:

1 You will learn from the ups and downs of students on their PhD journey and how they overcame their obstacles
2 You will be able to reflect on their choices or actions and consider your next step
3 You will discover proven ways adopted by those who achieved their much sought-after PhD
4 You will discover the crucial reasons why some students spend more years on the programme
5 Supervisors will be challenged to empathize with students – strengthening that necessary learning bond
6 Supervisors will see the practical challenges faced by many PhD students from across the globe

Overview

This book is about my personal PhD journey as an international student. Of course, my experience will differ from yours because we are unique individuals from different backgrounds. Nonetheless, each of us can learn from the road maps drawn by others. By avoiding the pitfalls cited in this book and taking note of the informed choices of others, we can make informed decisions that will help us to succeed on the PhD journey.

The book targets international students studying in the United Kingdom (UK) and includes my conversations with PhD students and graduates from Jordan, Uzbekistan, Nigeria, Cameroon, Angola, China and India. Seven interviewees had successfully earned their PhDs (2017/2019) and ten were completing their final year (2019/2020). The PhD students and graduates were selected from the

University of Manchester, Cardiff Metropolitan University, Coventry University, Anglia Ruskin University and the University of Leeds.

Because I had earned my PhD from Cardiff Metropolitan University, it might have been easier to interview more students from my university. However, I wanted to avoid having a single perspective by choosing only one university, so I extended my search to include PhD students and graduates from other universities. Therefore, to increase my sample, I requested assistance from my interviewees, who were able to suggest friends who would be interested in sharing their experiences.

Of interest are the individual stories of each. The road to graduation took the same direction, but the paving was different – each had so much to share! I found their unique narratives fascinating. Their lessons, from whichever year they recounted, offered so much that was helpful. I found myself thinking, 'If only I had known this before, then . . .'. I now know what the old saying, 'Before you criticize anyone, walk a mile in their shoes' really means. Interviews were conducted over the phone because it was more convenient for busy students.

I explained the purpose of my research – to include their stories in a book I was writing and that there was also the possibility that supervisors might read it and gain a clearer picture of what their students might be going through. Of course, each participant received the assurance that their confidentiality and anonymity would be protected. Each interview followed a semi-structured style (question–answer–discussion) and lasted around 65 minutes. Paraphrases of the interview notes and verbatim quotes feature in this book. I recall, with gratitude, the passionate and constructively delivered narrative from each participant. I have used fictitious names to guarantee anonymity. Below are examples of the interview questions from which their respective stories have been shared.

Examples of the questions

1 Why did you embark on a PhD journey, or Why did you choose to do a PhD?
2 What were your initial fears or concerns when you started, or were about to start, your PhD?
3 What is/was the toughest part of your PhD journey?
4 How is/was your relationship with your supervisor? Or was/is your supervisor helpful on your journey?
5 What advice would you give to anyone who wants to start a PhD?
6 In hindsight, what would you do differently if you were to start your PhD again? Knowing all that you have known, if you were to start a PhD again, what would you change or do differently?

Now, let's turn to the PhD stories from successful students – and those still on their journey.

International students' experiences

Mimi's PhD journey

Mimi, a PhD graduate, has shared her five years' journey on her programme. She established a consulting firm after completing a master's degree. Mimi soon discovered that, as a consultant offering professional advice, many of her clients expected her to have earned a doctorate. So, to ensure the sustainability of her enterprise, she enrolled at a UK university. She identified a gap (unaddressed challenges) in her industry, and this became the focus of her research.

Nonetheless, Mimi was afraid she might not get a competent supervisor. She had heard about some problems caused by supervisors. Also, Mimi was concerned about the length of time required for the course. However, she ended up with two fantastic supervisors who met her needs for guidance on her research and knowledge in her chosen field of study. Also, Mimi was to learn many crucial lessons and, by learning from the guidance of her focused supervisors, she began her journey.

Lesson one unfolded when Mimi discovered that her supervisors were not impressed with her methodology chapter. She then realized the need to humble herself and take on board the knowledge and expertise of her capable supervisors. You see, while Mimi was competent in report writing, she had no idea of one of the critical skills needed – academic writing. So, during the relearning process, she grasped the difference between report writing and academic writing for a thesis.

Lesson two. Mimi was not entitled to support from the British government. Consequently, she had to plan her work–life balance. Fortuitously, her supervisory team understood and accommodated her need to address her financial needs. So, meeting deadlines became the crucial markers along her journey, and when she could not meet the occasional deadline, she would consult with her professors and reschedule. Not all supervisors are unsympathetic to genuine student needs.

Lesson three. Mimi hit the buffers of UK immigration policy. She explained:

> The policy makes it look like becoming pregnant is a crime if you are a PhD student. If you are pregnant, you will be required to go back to your home country if you wanted to take maternity leave of over four weeks. Then when your maternity leave is over, you can come back to your studies. Considering that I had another child who was already in school would mean that I will have to take him out of school if I was required to leave. This will lead to some unnecessary travel expenses for my family and me.

However, Mimi had to swallow the reality pill. It was not wise to challenge the legal constraints of her host country and so she completed her PhD within five years. She accepted challenges as opportunities to learn how to adapt, rather than dead-end markers.

Mimi has offered helpful advice. She recommends you have a good understanding of research methods and methodology. You should research your potential supervisors, so you know about their work and research approach. Remember that supervisors are busy people and to get the best out of them will require a commitment on your part. If you prove to your supervisors that you are committed, they will support you. Furthermore, she suggests that you keep track of your written changes and save all copies. Set up a recording system that, for example, contains your portfolio for Year One, Year Two, and so on, to help you recollect what you have achieved each year. Finally, back up your work immediately – be proactive, and remember Murphy's Law: 'If anything can go wrong, it will.'

Anna's PhD journey

Anna is in the final year of a doctorate and has spent seven years on a programme that is only supposed to take four.

The toughest parts of Anna's PhD journey cover four areas.

Firstly, Anna is a young mother of three, struggling with her study–family balance.

Secondly, Anna was on a student visa that was valid for only three years. When her visa expired, the Home Office refused her visa extension application. Sadly, Anna became depressed. This prevented her from completing her research within the standard three-year period. Also, she was constrained financially because she lost her right to work in the UK following her visa extension refusal. This made Anna abandon her research because she was not in a good state of mind to continue. She needed a valid leave to remain visa to be able to complete her studies. Anna knew that if she returned to her home country she would not be able to complete her programme because some of the facilities needed to conduct her research would not be readily available.

To compound her problems, Anna's university was not supportive. They threatened her with reminder emails that she would be withdrawn from the programme if she did not have a valid visa. The school did not provide her with a letter to extend her visa.

Let us read what Anna experienced. 'The university left me with no choice than to abandon the PhD. I began to look for another visa route. I have my visa. I am back. I am about to complete my research in preparation for the final viva. However, this has come at a huge cost.'

Thirdly, Anna's supervisor was not always around. He was incommunicado for about nine months. When he eventually became available, he made Anna start her research afresh because she was heading in the wrong direction. Although, her supervisor supported her with materials and useful feedback, the problem was the time it took him to respond because of his busy schedule.

Though her relationship with her supervisor was cordial, she was not motivated to put in much effort because she was not encouraged by his prolonged absence. It was during her studies that she gave birth to a third child, and as she was struggling to balance her school and family life her supervisor advised her to focus on her family first. According to her supervisor, 'You don't do a PhD under stress. You need to be relaxed to produce a quality thesis.' Anna's supervisor was considerate because of her circumstances (pregnancy, visa and family).

Fourthly, Anna did not have ready access to academic journals. Most of the academic journals required payment before she could access articles, so she was relying mostly on free journals to save cost.

Anna offered the following advice to anyone wishing to undertake a PhD:

- You need to be prepared. You need to have a 'go-for-it attitude' if you really want to succeed.
- A PhD is not a one-year or two-year journey. Life situations will kick in. At some point, you will feel like you do not want to carry on.
- It's better to have your supervisor readily available. It will save you a lot of time and stress.
- Make sure your research is done where you can access data taking into consideration your geographical location.

Fazil's PhD journey

Fazil began working on his PhD in 2013, and is now in his final year. He had wanted to be able to stay in the UK legally, and the PhD was the route to extending his visa. Fazil spent a long time deciding on an appropriate research topic but, once he put pen to paper, he faced problems! He was not going to have a comfortable ride.

Fazil's first challenge was not academic but supervision.

My supervisors both had a qualitative research background. They made me focus on their own area of specialization. When I got stuck, they did not help me. They said I should find textbooks on statistics that will address my concerns. They said a PhD is an independent study. They said it's not their fault that I did not understand statistics. I became depressed following these comments, and I wrote to the university to withdraw from the programme. Thankfully, the PhD programme administrator reached out to me and advised me not to withdraw. So, after three months of not doing anything, I received the support of the PhD programme administrator. The only way I overcame my depression was the professional support I received from the senior academic adviser. Because I had withdrawn, the supervisors took on new students and no longer had my time. So we began looking for another supervisor. This time, I got a supervisor who was very helpful and had good knowledge of data analysis using statistical tools. So, my new supervisor's expertise in my research area made me progress quickly.

Fazil's second challenge was about data collection. He was very enthusiastic but was not realistic in terms of his sample. He explained that he collected data

from 400 people whereas about 45 professionals' opinions would have been enough. Consequently, he had to spend around six months analysing his data.
So, what can Fazil teach us?

- I would recommend all international students whose first language is not English to get a minimum IELTS (International English Language Testing System) score of 7 in Writing. The university I attended recommended 6, but that is not enough to overcome the complexities that arise during the writing stage of research.
- I would advise PhD students to use more 'in-house' supervisors – i.e. supervisors from the institution they are studying at. These academics have a duty to uphold the reputation of the university. I would not recommend contractual supervisors. Sometimes they have too many students from their university and other institutions. The university cannot control their workload. As a result, they are less likely to be available to help students – unlike in-house supervisors.
- If I had the opportunity to start all over, I would consider sending my family back to my home country for a few years during my PhD. If you are here alone without your family, you will be more focused on your study. Family can be a distraction. You unexpectedly spend more time and money than you think. For example, I had to work full time to be able to raise money for living expenses for my family while applying to extend my visa, and this delayed my research.

Zaki's PhD journey

Zaki is a PhD graduate who completed his programme in three years. He lectures at a university in his home country. Zaki said that earning his PhD was the key to his academic career as a lecturer. Nonetheless, he had to work through some concerns.

In his first year, he did not know what the focus of his research should be. In his second year, he had concerns about his social life – he had no family, and wanted to marry. A wife would bring added joy to his otherwise mundane academic life. In fact, he was becoming bored with books, journals and essays.

So, what did he do to get back on track and refocus on his career-enhancing directive? Let us read how Zaki turned himself around. The crucial factor is that he took responsibility to change and renew his motivation. This reminds me that we are responsible for our own career.

'Regarding my focus, I was trying to develop a tool but was not getting the results I wanted. There was so much pressure from my supervisor to get it done. But after repeated attempts, I successfully developed the software, then I became calm, and my supervisor was equally happy. With respect to my private–academic life conundrum, I travelled home to meet my family, and this kind of refreshed me.'

Zaki was able to publish some articles, but he also had to sort out the data-collection process and carefully select the data he needed. He has offered some useful advice. He says, 'Doing a PhD must be a personal decision, and not because you want to be called a 'Dr'. Furthermore, a PhD is a tough journey, and you must always remember this.'

Iram's PhD journey

Iram is a PhD graduate who completed her programme in three years. Because she had already studied at master's level in the UK, she was culturally aware of her environment and knew what to expect.

For Iram, earning a PhD was an exciting and different academic journey. She had been told that a PhD can take from seven to ten years to complete. However, she had wondered why a three-year programme could take seven years. Nevertheless, Iram made a commitment to be disciplined, to focus and work hard. She made sure she doubled her efforts to succeed – including putting in extra study hours. As she did not have a family with her it was easier to devote the bulk of her time to study. She studied full time and worked part time for 20 hours a week.

Iram explained that the most frustrating and demanding stage of her PhD was the extra effort and time doing data analysis. She used the NVivo tool, but because she manually transcribed all her interviews this made it the most challenging aspect of her research.

So, what lessons can we learn from Iram's three-year PhD journey?

Lesson one: Iram had an excellent relationship with her supervisor, and this contributed to completing her research on time. Her supervisor was very supportive and always followed up on her progress to ensure that she submitted her draft chapters based on the timelines they had agreed.

Lesson two: she learnt that great people learn from other people, so she made sure she spoke to those who had begun a PhD before her. She shared her concerns, and their advice helped her to avoid specific problems.

Lesson three: she participated in the peer-review committee. This helped her to discuss her research concerns. The comments and contributions from supervisors and other PhD students helped her progress.

Iram has offered the following helpful advice to anyone wishing to undertake PhD study:

- You should be mentally and emotionally prepared.
- The research area you are working on should be something you are passionate about so that, even if you are bored, the interest will inspire you.
- Make sure you have an excellent relationship with your supervisor.
- Doing a PhD means you are adding a value that has not been there before. It could be newness of approach, knowledge, research, process or methods.

Esi's PhD journey

Esi is a final-year PhD student and has spent seven years on her programme. She was raised to value education and wanted to get to the peak of academia. Esi has two master's degrees. Initially she was not sure what she wanted to focus on for her PhD research. She thought about extending her research from her master's degree in sociology, but could not come up with a research problem. Esi began to think of an area that would be interesting and something that would lead her to the next phase of her life. She loves fashion, arts and music, and so decided to choose a topic that would align with these and satisfy her passion for creativity.

Despite her strong academic background, Esi was nervous when starting her PhD. She questioned why she wanted to gain the degree and wondered whether her research would merit a PhD. She was worried about the number of years she had invested in education. She had spent four years on undergraduate study (bachelor's degree), two years on postgraduate study (master's degrees), and the thought of another three to four years for a doctoral degree was scary. Esi spoke to others already doing their PhDs, and they advised her to take one day at a time. Her biggest problem was the writing process, structuring her work and managing her time.

Then the unexpected crossed Esi's path: her beloved father died during her second year – the crucial period for collecting data. She could not deal with her grief and became depressed and demoralized for three years. Fortunately, her partner's support and her supervisor's empathy led to a full recovery after her extension of time ended.

Later, Esi's supervisor became pregnant and took leave of absence. The new supervisor and Esi failed to bond. However, Esi had to put up with her. Let us read her words.

> I would have changed her from the beginning, but she was appointed in the middle of my research, so I had to endure her. I believed that I could still learn from someone that I cannot stand. I had to put up with her because I must, not because I wanted her to supervise my work. She was very annoying. She started requesting changes in my work which meant changing my entire topic after researching for four years. I felt she did not have my interest at heart and was trying to mislead me. Each time she asked me to create a new chapter, for example, and I ended up with twenty chapters. I wished I had changed this second supervisor from the beginning because I had a colleague who changed her supervisor, and now she has completed her research within four years.

Esi recommends that when considering embarking on a PhD study, you should choose a subject that interests you – something you will be passionate about – and you should consider how you can access data. Because of her experience, she suggests that you talk to your supervisor about any problems, sometimes informally.

Themes from interview questions

1 Why did you embark on a PhD journey, or Why did you choose to do a PhD?
   - Societal expectation/client expectation
   - Seeking solution to a problem/to solve a problem
   - To extend my visa

- Requirement for my lecturing career
- Personal and professional development
- To change my career
- Family pressure

2 What were your initial fears or concerns when you started, or were about to start, your PhD?
- Possibility of not getting a good supervisor
- Study duration
- Financial constraints/funding challenges
- Choosing an appropriate research area/topic
- Managing my time
- Whether my work will be up to PhD standard

3 What is/was the toughest part of your PhD journey?
- Thesis writing/academic writing
- Work–life balance
- Immigration-related problems/problems with visa extensions
- Manual transcription of data
- Financial constraint/funding
- Lack of access to academic journals
- Supervisor was incommunicado
- Supervisor not knowledgeable in research area and not supportive
- Supervisor supportive but not knowledgeable in research area
- Data collection – sample size was too large and time-consuming to analyse
- Lost my dad – this led to mental health problems, and it took me three years to return to my research
- Change of supervisor in the middle of my study

4 How is/was your relationship with your supervisor? Or was/is your supervisor helpful on your journey?
- Fantastic relationship – supervisor knowledgeable in my research area
- Excellent relationship – supervisor very supportive
- Good relationship – but supervisor was incommunicado most of the time
- Bad relationship – supervisory team not knowledgeable in my research area and unsupportive
- Bad relationship – supervisor did not have my interest at heart – I was enduring my supervisor

5 What advice would you give to anyone who wants to start a PhD?
- Research your supervisor
- Learn from other student–supervisor relationships
- Prove to supervisors you are committed
- Keep track of all changes to your work
- Keep copies of your work

- Be prepared mentally and emotionally
- Research on a subject you are passionate about
- Speak to and learn from PhD students ahead of you
- Participate in peer-review committees
- Consider your location and whether you can access data
- If English is not your first language, you should aim to have an IELTS score of 7 in Writing – students will struggle if they get a lower Writing score
- Embarking on a PhD must be a personal decision – otherwise you may become overwhelmed and tired
- It's an independent/lone journey, so try to get personal satisfaction
- Talk to your supervisor about any problems (sometimes informally)

6   In hindsight, what would you do differently if you were to start your PhD again? Knowing all that you have known, if you were to start a PhD again, what would you change or do differently?

- I would consider attending more academic seminars and research training
- I would consider sending my family back to my home country so I can focus more on my study
- I would consider getting two years' work experience in a related field before embarking on my research
- I would manage my time better

Conclusions and recommendations from the interviews

A doctorate is quite an emotional undertaking filled with dilemmas and frustrating dead-ends. However, despite vast research on how to achieve a successful PhD, there seems to be little in its content that empathizes with international students who, on their academic journey, seek to navigate and adapt to the culture and legislation of their host country and university. This research examined several challenges faced by international students undertaking a doctoral degree at universities in the UK. Seventeen participants comprising ten final-year PhD students and seven recent PhD graduates were interviewed over a period of four months. A thematic analysis of the interviews revealed that: (1) most students residing in the UK with their families took longer to complete the doctorate, which was due to them balancing study time with working long hours in order to meet their families' financial needs; (2) immigration restrictions accounted for an astounding 80 per cent of the emotional distress experienced by PhD students, often leading to either prolonged years of study or academic withdrawal; (3) having a supervisor who supported students as well as empathized with them accounted for around 90 per cent of the overall academic success and subsequent graduation. It is hoped that the second finding emerging from these interviews will encourage the UK Visas and Immigration (UKVI) division of the Home Office to debate a visa policy that meets the needs of doctoral students and is separate from a Tier 4 (General) student visa. A full-time PhD takes between three and four years to complete, depending on the academic institution. With that in mind, it would be of great benefit to grant, for instance, a five-year (PhD) student visa, thus bringing much-needed reassurance about course completion at doctorate level, and promoting the continuing, supportive and all-inclusive nature of the host country.

It must also be mentioned that a number of doctoral students attributed some of their challenges in part to lack of support from their supervisors. Hence, supervisors and universities need to recognize that international students face many difficulties, ranging from adjusting to a new environment and culture to learning independently. Furthermore, pastoral care should rest not only with the supervisors but the PhD programme administrators as well.

Areas of further research

As may be the case with any research, it is not without its limitations. Firstly, with qualitative research such as this, it is not entirely possible to provide statistical representation that is all-encompassing. Therefore, research which adopts mixed methods may offer a better overview and greater insight. Secondly, the given analysis focused on challenges experienced by international students studying in the UK and did not take into consideration experiences shared by home students. To further enhance the value of the available research, interviews could be conducted with a group of home students to identify their challenges. The results would offer themselves to comparison with the suggested findings of the existing research. A later, globally cascaded comparison could be achieved through identifying challenges experienced by international students in other countries. For instance, research findings and conclusions from academic institutions in Canada, the United States or Australia would provide valuable additions to the extant literature, so as to guide prospective international students, universities, supervisors and government immigration departments on the necessary proactive steps, thus mitigating an emotionally overwhelming doctoral journey (Iornem, K.S. 2020).

Chapter 1: summary

Chapter 1 presented the ups and downs of students on their PhD journey and how they overcame the hurdles the faced. The research findings revealed the crucial reasons why some students spend more years completing the programme than others. The chapter presented the author's recommendations in light of the findings and suggested areas of further research and development.

In Chapter 2, we will explore some of the fears that students express when embarking on a PhD journey. The author shares his motivational experience while completing his PhD and hopes the section will inspire readers to overcome their concerns.

2 Concerns, reservations and fears about starting a PhD

By the end of this chapter, you will be able to:

1 Explain your motivation for doing a PhD
2 Outline your progress plan
3 Plan your schedule

Introduction

Very few people make impulsive decisions to begin a PhD. Some have no idea about how they will manage the challenge. The excitement of embarking on a doctoral study could be, for example, because of career opportunities, academic advancement, or an interest in unravelling a research problem. Others may want to do a PhD to confirm, counter or extend existing research, gain recognition within the community, or because of family or peer pressure. Whatever the reasons, the main challenges students face at the initial stage include trying to select an appropriate topic, defining the problem, asking the right research questions, and so on.

Others have reservations – as had I. My dated knowledge of statistics raised red flags about how prepared I was. Then there are those who fear the unknown and do not understand the strange new world that includes the need to test a hypothesis, focus on academic writing, avoid plagiarism, and the all-important financial outlay. So, if you are in a quandary – welcome to the PhD Club!

Having earned my MBA and MSc, I spent one year procrastinating and mulling over proceeding to a PhD. Eventually, having cleared away the negatives (e.g. funding challenges and finalizing my research proposal) I applied to the university and was soon face to face with my interviewer, who began to ask questions.

1 'Why do you want to earn a PhD?' In other words, what was my motivation?

I gave two salient reasons – my desire to bring change to an aspect of my country's education system and my need to establish my academic credentials in my work situation. I then shared the broad idea of 'the problem' that had caused ongoing hassle in tertiary education:

> I am interested in and very passionate about my country's development. You see, as a student back in the days at Ahmadu Bello University, I experienced several industrial actions by the Academic Staff Union of Universities. The disruptions led to the closure of our school, and I had to spend extra years completing my course. To date, many students suffer the same fate because of similar strike actions – across Nigeria. Thus, because of lecturers' job dissatisfaction, student learning is affected.
>
> We are aware that when people are not happy with their jobs, they tend to find alternative employment, or they reduce their commitment to their current job. In some cases, the employee leaves the organization. Consequently, the organization may incur costs in recruiting and training new staff – in addition to the hiatus of service caused by a resignation.
>
> Lecturers are essential stakeholders in a country's growth and development. They help in the field of research, prepare individuals for employment, and disseminate knowledge. They are critical players in the field of education.
>
> So, I am motivated to research an answer to this educational conundrum. Is there an alternative management model that Nigerian universities can adopt to better shape their human resource policies and practices to reduce the turnover of lecturers?

From answering the 'why' – my motivation – the interviewer then needed to know 'what' I had in mind.

2 'How will your proposed plan link to others in the same or a related field?'

I then outlined my idea, introduced the theories and methodologies I had in mind, and left the interview feeling like I had won the lottery. I was on my way to a new chapter in my life. I had permission to begin my PhD.

Four years later I was capped! However, I had to plan my programme to accommodate my prime needs and responsibilities, with these questions in mind:

1 Would I study full time or part time?
2 How could I manage family and personal commitments?
3 What known health issues needed navigating?
4 What about budget needs?
5 As a foreign student, could I meet the UK student visa conditions?
6 How would I keep focused and motivated?
7 What was the best way to manage my time?
8 How could I improve my data-collection skills?

9 How would I handle the expected criticisms from my supervisors?

10 Who could I look to for support, and also be accountable to for my progress?

Of course, individuals will have their own 'Progress Agenda' to consider. However, I reminded myself of the adage, 'If you fail to plan, you plan to fail'. Being realistic, pragmatic and sensible helps to pave the way. The only difference between you and me is that my concerns were successfully addressed, my reservations sorted out, and my fears laid to rest. You, too, can experience the joy and triumph of success!

Suggestions

Success is earned. So, why not talk to those who have completed their PhD journey and ask them about the following milestones that await you:

1 Supervision
2 Research difficulties
3 Career advancement
4 Social recognition
5 Peer learning
6 Using the library
7 Employing the services of a competent proofreader and editor
8 Observing university criteria
9 Keeping your balance and dealing with setbacks
10 Remaining focused

Chapter 2: summary

This chapter explained some of the fears that students express when embarking on a PhD journey. The author shared his motivational experience while completing his PhD and hopes to inspire readers to overcome their concerns.

In Chapter 3, we will explore ways to ensure that your research is unique. In addition, the guidelines from the UK Quality Code for Higher Education for awarding a PhD will help you on your journey.

The PhD journey in summary – from start to finish

By the end of this chapter, you will be able to:

1 List the entry requirements for doing a PhD
2 Develop an outline for the research proposal
3 Explain the stages you will need to pass through on your research journey

Funding

A PhD journey is very demanding, but it can also be exciting, especially if you can worry less about funding. This section aims to share a range of funding sources so that you can think less about financing when you eventually start your PhD. Unlike other postgraduate courses, a PhD is an expensive programme, be it part-time or full-time study. It is even more costly if you are studying at a university as an international student. In the UK, the cost of PhD full-time study is from as low as £18,000 (if you are studying via an affiliate institution) to as high as £50,000, depending on the course and university. This can be expensive for a private individual. Most commonly you need to consider scholarship opportunities, but these can be limited and sometimes only available for more specialized courses or science-related disciplines. Therefore, you need to work out how you would raise the money to pay your fees.

Most PhD students support themselves through a combination of personal savings, family help or loans. However, there are a wide range of funding sources for fees and living expenses available. Many – especially international students – take part-time work to help cover their tuition and living expenses, but this may not be enough to sustain you for the duration of the course. Knowledge is power, so knowing that funding opportunities are available is the first step in the right direction, and this can offer the hope which will inspire you to search for these opportunities. Lukins (2018) lists the familiar sources of PhD funding, including crowdfunding, employer funding, postgraduate loans, studentships, research council grants and charities.

PhD funding sources

1 Research council grant

Available to UK and European Union (EU) citizens. If you are from the UK or EU, you should consider this as your priority. One of the advantages is that you do not have to repay it. The grant would typically cover you for the duration of your course, but may also depend on your academic performance on the programme.

2 Postgraduate loan

If you are a UK or EU national resident in the UK, you may be able to secure a postgraduate loan of up to £25,000. An advantage of this funding source is that your financial status is not relevant before borrowing the money.

3 Employer sponsorship

Some employees get support from their employers. In most instances, this will be available if the course is going to be beneficial to the organization. However, to benefit from such funding you must be sure that the financial opportunity exists, and in many cases it is not automatic. You will need to submit a proposal to secure consideration by the company. Make sure to include the cost, duration, area of specialization, a clear explanation of why you are embarking on the study programme, and the potential benefits to your employer.

4 Studentship

Studentships are a popular source of funding throughout the world. Studentship and PhD scholarships are often used interchangeably and mean the same thing. Many universities offer various scholarships, and this lifts the financial burden from students. Some of these scholarships cover science, technology, engineering and medicine subjects (STEM). Some studentships – for example, at the London School of Economics – cover full tuition fees and an annual allowance of £18,000. Many students would not have been able to complete their PhD programme without a studentship. Furthermore, there is great joy derived from this funding opportunity as it allows you to focus on your study without worrying about your next supply of cash.

5 Crowdfunding

Some see this funding opportunity as a last resort, especially as it means asking for assistance from family and friends, and sometimes even strangers. Though this can seem extreme, Lukins (2018) recommends you keep this option open. Seeking funding via this source would mean that you should be able to justify why people should contribute towards your studies, especially as you would be the sole beneficiary.

6 Charities

Charities may be able to offer a funding opportunity. However, be aware that as they have many projects to embark on, they might not cover your entire costs. Lukins (2018) suggests that you may be able to combine multiple sources of funds – referred to as 'portfolio funding' – to be able to get sufficient money to cover part, or all, of your tuition, and perhaps your living expenses.

In general, to access scholarship opportunities, I would recommend you carry out a simple Google search like 'PhD funding opportunities in the UK'. You will come across many resources – check if you are eligible. You can also do a similar search for any country or subject-specific course.

The application and entry requirements

Different schools have different requirements. It is up to you to research the specific institution to see their admission requirements and guidelines for writing proposals.

Master's degree: A standard prerequisite for many universities is a master's degree with a minimum of a merit grade. Other universities vary and may accept a lower pass percentage if the applicant can demonstrate that he/she is competent in research methods and has a proposal that can lead to a theoretical and practical contribution. Please contact the respective universities to find out their specific entry requirements.

Competency in the English language: A good command of English is an essential requirement for most universities. In the UK, students who come from countries whose official language is not English will be required to demonstrate competence in the English language via tests such as IELTS (International English Language Testing System) and TOEFL (Test of English as a Foreign Language). IELTS and TOEFL scores are recognized by more than 10,000 universities and other education providers in over 150 countries, including Australia, Canada, New Zealand, the UK, the United States, and across Europe and Asia (www.ielts.org; www.ets.org). The exact entry score varies from university to university, and I would advise you look up the entry requirements for each university through their admissions department.

Proposal and personal statement: Applicants are required to submit a research proposal and, in some instances, a motivation statement.

Research proposal writing

A proposal is a summary of your planned research work and a vital part of your research. I want you to think of your proposal as a Google Map. You want to move from Point A to Point B. You can walk, take a cab, a train, or you can cycle. Which option works best for you considering the resources available? Also, there are different routes. Which route should you use? Why should you use that route? The idea is that, if you plan your journey considering the alternatives and challenges you may experience (for example, road closure) you will be able to get to your destination with less hassle than if you did not map out your journey planner from the onset. This is precisely how a proposal helps you to achieve your research objectives. Universities have different guidelines for writing proposals. The word count varies from 1,000 to 2,500 words, depending on the institution.

I recommend that you strictly adhere to each institution's requirements (for example, the word count, structure, referencing style, and so on).

However, intakes for PhD programmes can sometimes be limited (occasionally due to supervisor unavailability). Therefore, you may want to submit proposals to several universities while adjusting the proposals to meet each institution's proposal specification. As template and word count requirements vary from institution to institution, I would advise you to adopt the template with the higher word count. This is because you will find it easier to reduce the word count to meet the requirements of another university instead of conducting additional research for a proposal with a higher word count.

As a guide, your doctoral research proposal might usefully be organized into ten sections:

1 **Introduction**

   A clear statement about what you want to work on and why it is necessary, interesting, relevant and realistic.

2 **Statement of the problem**

   What is the main issue? What are you trying to address? What is the puzzle?

3 **Purpose, objectives and rationale of the study**

   What are your main research objectives? – these could be articulated as hypotheses, propositions, research questions or problems to solve. Your research objectives and/or questions should be kept to a minimum – no more than five objectives or questions.

4 **The significance of the study (including a mention of those who will benefit)**

   How will your research 'add value' to the subject, and who – which people or organizations – will benefit from your research?

5 **Previous research and developments in this field of study**

   Some background knowledge and context of the area in which you wish to work, including crucial literature, relevant people and pertinent research findings.

   How does your work link to the work of others in the same or related fields?

6 **Research methods or procedures that you intend to use – i.e. library research, empirical research – including a brief mention of the intended research instruments**

   How will you conduct your research?

   Will you use existing theories, methods/approaches or develop new methods/approaches?

   How will you design your project to get the best results/findings?

7 **Tentative hypotheses**

   What will the study try to show or prove?

8 **Expected findings (if possible)**

   What are the possible outcomes of your research considering your statement of the problem, objectives and questions?

9 **Tentative conclusions and implications**

Are there any theoretical implications or practical implications?

10 **References**

A list of the critical references which support your research proposal.

Contacting potential supervisors

After you have considered the funding alternatives, and drafted your research proposal, you can start looking up the universities that have supervisors in your research area. You should consider looking up and adhering to the university's proposal writing guidelines.

Look up the supervisors in the subject area you are interested in. The supervisors normally have information about their research interests available on the university's page in the respective department. Try contacting a potential supervisor by email with your research topic and a summary of your proposal to see if he/she is available and interested. The content of the email is very important: remember that supervisors are busy people, so try to get straight to the point – in a polite manner. Check spelling and grammar in your cover letter. First impressions count.

University College London (UCL) provides useful tips on how to contact a potential supervisor. If you follow them, you will improve your chances of a successful application. You will also likely get the most appropriate supervisor to meet your research needs. When making a research enquiry, remember that academics usually have tight schedules. Research suggests that 67 per cent of supervisors are contacted with research enquiries that are not related to their fields. Therefore, make sure you thoroughly research the potential supervisor's interests before contacting them. In some cases, they may not have time to reply to your query, especially if it is unrelated to their research interests.

UCL provides further helpful information on how to contact supervisors for your research interests:

- When writing an email, make sure you focus on your strengths.
- Ensure that your grammar is good. Check it carefully and avoid spelling mistakes.
- Just as, when applying for work, you have different CVs tailored for different jobs, it is best to use different emails for different supervisors. You should edit your existing template to include the research interests of the different academics, and refer to their recent work when you contact them.

You should include important information such as:

- the funding status
- your status – either a UK, international or EU student
- whether you want to study full time or part time.

Supervisors in different fields and institutions have their own unique requirements. Notwithstanding, they would usually expect you to highlight your research interest and include a brief motivation statement. Furthermore, supervisors expect to see a professionally written proposal related to recent research they have conducted (University College London, n.d.).

The interview

Basically, though universities requirements vary, what they want to establish includes:

- Your motivation for doing a PhD.
- What support you have – for example, funding, research methods training, and so on?
- That you are a genuine student with an interest and passion, as they would not want someone to come and waste their time and money. Doing a PhD is a serious business.
- That you have a clear research question and have thought about the approach to answering it.
- That you can explain its significance and how it could contribute to the body of knowledge.
- That you can explain the importance of the proposed study, and why you are the right candidate to undertake it.

Upgrade or transfer to a PhD

When you are admitted, you are initially registered on an MPhil/PhD programme. After the first or second year, you will be assessed and then upgraded to PhD status if you satisfy the examiners. If they think your work will not meet the standards set for a PhD (original contribution), you may be advised to proceed to complete an MPhil degree instead (which will typically take around 12 to 24 months to finish).

Annual monitoring report (AMR)

This is a discussion and milestone check between the trio – the student and the two supervisors. It is conducted every year to check the progress, challenges and work to be done by the student. A student who completes the PhD in three years would have completed the AMR1, AMR2 and AMR3 forms. If it is completed in four years, AMR4 will also need to be completed. The supervisors provide their recommendations, and the student is required to provide feedback on aspects of their research, including supervision, training, workspace, IT and library facilities, and so on. The form is submitted to the school's Research Degree Committee for their necessary approval and action.

Mock viva

This is usually conducted internally by the university when you have completed all your chapters, in preparation for the final viva. The mock viva is similar to the final viva, except the outcome is not the final decision. It is intended to help you shape your work and address any gaps. The examiners give you their assessment of the shortcomings in your thesis and suggest ways you can improve it. They also try to establish that you have adequate knowledge of the subject area, including the principal authors who have influenced your work, and that you have applied the appropriate research methods.

Viva voce

Usually about three to four months before the final submission of your work, you would be required to discuss with your supervisory team and then complete the necessary forms for submission. Your supervisory team would then be required to source an external examiner in your proposed research area and get their detailed CV. It is good practice to discuss this with your supervisory team so you can begin to consider looking up the potential external examiner's publications. This information might be beneficial to your thesis.

When the forms have been completed, submitted and approved by the relevant department, the institution will be required to officially invite the examiners by providing them with your abstract. When the examiners confirm that they can act, and a date has been agreed for the viva examinations, they would be sent a copy of your thesis.

When you finish your viva, the outcome will be one of the six listed:

1   You pass without any correction – this rarely happens.
2   You pass with minor corrections – you will be given about three months within which to revise and resubmit your work.
3   You pass with major corrections – a second viva may be scheduled, for which you will be granted about 12 months to make the necessary changes to your work and resubmit it.
4   You fail, but the examiners recommend you for an MPhil award.
5   You fail, but the examiners recommend you for an MPhil award, subject to minor corrections – you will be given about three months to make the changes and resubmit your work.
6   You fail – your work does not merit even an MPhil.

The university will then officially write to you regarding the oral examination to confirm the outcome and offer guidance on the next process, including a list of the agreed corrections to be made and a table to demonstrate those corrections.

On satisfactory completion, you will be required to submit two bound copies and a soft copy in line with your university's guidelines for formatting and binding. There are usually submission deadlines, and you need to adhere to these or you might incur expenses for an extension. The Research Degree Committee will review and confirm your corrections and you will be included on the list of graduands for the next graduation ceremony.

Chapter 3: summary

This chapter provided information about the cost of embarking on a PhD at specific UK institutions – for example, fees start from as low as £18,000 to as high as £50,000 for students from outside the EU.

The chapter explained the entry requirements, which include having a master's degree, showing evidence of competency in the English language, and submitting a personal statement and research proposal about your intended field of study. The content includes step-by-step information on what to expect on the PhD journey, from admission up to your final viva.

The next chapter explains the nature of a PhD in detail. It discusses how you can ensure your research meets the critical PhD criteria – making an original contribution to knowledge.

4 | What is a PhD?

By the end of this chapter, you will be able to:

1 Define a PhD
2 Explain what constitutes original research
3 Identify ways to contribute to the body of knowledge
4 Discuss how PhDs are awarded in the UK

> A PhD is a globally recognized postgraduate academic degree awarded by universities and higher education institutions to a candidate who has submitted a *thesis or dissertation,* based on extensive and original research in their chosen field (Haidar, 2020).

Thesis or dissertation?

The terms 'thesis' and 'dissertation', as highlighted in Haidar's definition above, are pretty much interchangeable – though, as Figure 1 points out, the meaning can vary between the United States and the UK (Enago, 2018).

Figure 1 Thesis or dissertation

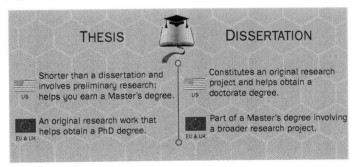

Enago, 2018

Original research explained

Having dealt with the semantics, let me explain the concept of original research as used in Haidar's definition of a PhD. I recall the memorable words of my programme leader, Nandish Patel, who explained that your data makes your research unique. But what does this mean?

1 Your sample may be a target population that other researchers may not have explored or considered. For example, previous research may have explored job satisfaction of academic staff at XYZ university. You may have an interest in job satisfaction and the turnover of employees and want to consider non-academic staff probably at XYZ university, or even academic staff at ABC university. Looking at the two scenarios, your sample is different and there are chances that your findings may be different.

2 Also, the method you use for collecting the data may be different from procedures used by other scholars. For example, a researcher may have collected quantitative data (survey, questionnaire). You might prefer a method that provides more insight to enable you to understand the issues in contention, and the only way to achieve this would be if you conducted in-depth interviews. Thus, your research will provide a different approach to explaining the data.

Caveat

Using a different method or a different sample does not necessarily imply originality. It is your justification of your choices that suggests originality. For example, you might explain the cons of a particular method that has been used by other researchers and then offer the strengths of your proposed method, or note that previous research used a sample size that you considered too small and not representative of the population, and you consequentially decided to use a more extensive sample size that is more representative of the population. So, aim for originality.

Four possible ways to develop originality

Consider the following four possible ways of developing originality in your research:

Method 1: The Critical Literature Review

1 You must have an interest in a subject area (e.g. human resource management, critical management studies, leadership and leadership development, entrepreneurship, international business and international management, and so on).

2 You must hone down on the specific topic of interest – e.g. job satisfaction, disruptive innovation, cultural diversity, small and medium-sized enterprises (SMEs), corporate sustainability and corporate social responsibility (CSR), and so on. Beware of being too all-embracing.

3 You must read journal articles in your areas of interest to understand both the facts in contention and factors requiring consideration.

4 You will need to identify the knowledge gap. The missing link. The unexplored area.

Method 2: The Further Research Method

1 Follow steps 1 to 3 in Method 1 above.

2 You will need to look up the most recent published peer-reviewed articles in that subject area. Remember that sometimes researchers have a section for 'areas of further research' that might provide information on what they have not covered, but which they consider useful to add to the body of knowledge. For example, see Chapter 1, page 11, "Areas of further research" for my recommendations for further research.

3 Remember, there may be some researchers who have provided updated research on the topic you are interested in. Therefore, seek the most recent publications to avoid duplication of research.

4 You may also discover other scholars addressing the gap in knowledge you are researching. However, always bear in mind that you must present an original research portfolio.

Method 3: The Replication

You can replicate a research study using:

1 Different method(s)/technique(s).

2 Different populations/samples.

3 Different theories or concepts.

4 Either of, or all of, the above to compare how your findings relate to literature by either supporting or disproving the works of others.

Method 4: The Observation or Problem Statement Method

1 You may have observed a problem or phenomenon within your organization, community or country that requires attention.

2 You will need to read up articles on the topic:
   • To understand the issues or the phenomenon.
   • To understand how others have approached it.
   • To explore why the problem still persists.
   • To explore ways of addressing the issue.

Caveat

Please note that the work must be significant. In other words, the content must be meaningful and beneficial to other scholars, organizations, or a group of individuals.

For your work to be relevant, you need to answer these questions:

1 What can others learn from my research?
2 How can my original contribution to the knowledge pool be used by others?
3 What could my research accomplish in the hands of others?
4 Who is my target audience and how will my research benefit the focus group?
5 Why should anyone be interested in my research?

Extensive research

In one of our research seminars, Professor Nandish Patel explained that a PhD is an extension of the Body of Knowledge, and illustrated this concept using the diagram below. The idea is closely related to Might's (2010) *The Illustrated*

Figure 2 PhD – an extension of the body of knowledge

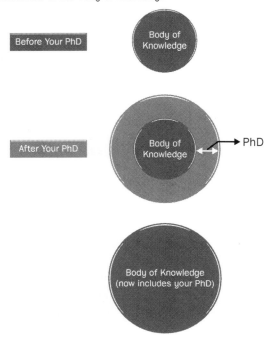

Guide to a Ph.D. So let us move on and discover the joy and discipline of this type of academic research.

1 Consider the first circle as what is already known research-wise – i.e. the existing literature, the existing body of knowledge.
2 Consider the second circle (with outer circle depicting a PhD) as the new knowledge you have added to the existing body of knowledge. This will become your unique contribution to knowledge (your PhD) that subsequently fills the knowledge gap.
3 Thereafter, your PhD – the Body of Knowledge – having filled the gap causes the area (the third circle) to expand and creates yet another circle waiting to be filled.

(A similar concept to Patel's class presentation.)

Now that we have dissected the definition of a PhD, I want to share the criteria for which some universities confer a PhD – based on the guidelines stipulated by the UK Quality Code for Higher Education.

The Doctor of Philosophy degree by Research is conferred by a university to students who successfully complete their doctoral programme and where, on the recommendation of the Research Degree Committee, the student's work contributes significantly to the body of knowledge. The student must demonstrate evidence of *systematic study* and the skills to link the results of such research to the extant literature on the subject (Cardiff Metropolitan University, 2018, p.4).

I have highlighted the phrase *systematic study*. I was asked during my mock viva to explain how I ensured my research was conducted systematically.

1 Consider answering the same question: How would you conduct a systematic study?
2 Have you answered the question?

My explanation was this:

How will you convince other scholars to believe your data and accept your findings in relation to your research area? The starting point is to gather information for your research. This includes:

1 Using key words to identify appropriate literature in your research field.
2 Citing credible sources.
3 Reviewing widely cited articles.
4 Citing articles from peer-reviewed journals.
5 Citing articles from journals with a high-impact factor.
6 Avoiding Wikipedia, some news sites and blogs, except if they are from an authoritative body – e.g. a government department providing, say, statistical information. Never use a source just because it is available. As you are dealing with data and will be having discussions and making conclusions

based on your findings, make sure you use reputable sources because if your data is unreliable (wrong), your findings will be skewed.

If you follow points 1 to 6, you will practise the discipline of being 'systematic'!
Now let us turn to your methodology, which explains why you have used certain tools or methods.

1 Which method do you want to employ to collect your data – e.g. survey using a questionnaire, interviews, case study, mixed methods (i.e. both survey and interviews), and so on?
2 What are your reasons for choosing the method?
3 What other possible methods could you have used, and why did you not use them?
4 What kind of questions should you ask?
5 Who are, or what is, your sample? – in other words, the group of people, objects or items you have selected from a larger population to analyse (The Hillingdon Hospital, 2006).
6 Why have you selected them?
7 How did you select them or how will you select them?
8 How many people or objects did you select?
9 Do you know the total population of the group of people or objects?
10 Is your selection representative of the population?
11 Can you use your results to subsequently generalize?

For researchers to believe your results, the instruments you use need to be valid and reliable as this will determine the quality of the investigation. An instrument is reliable when it produces a constant outcome (Kidder and Judd, 1986). On the other hand, the validity of a test instrument is the degree to which the test instrument measures exactly what it is designed to measure (Ogunleye, 2000).

Both reliability and validity need to go hand in hand to produce a realistic picture of your data. You can have a reliable instrument that is not valid. And you can have a valid instrument that is not reliable. For example, if your scale is off by 5 kg, it reads your weight every day with an excess of 5 kg. The scale is reliable because it consistently reports the same weight every day, but it is not valid because it adds 5 kg to your true weight. Therefore, it is not a valid measure of your weight.

As an example, let us use Brexit to explain validity. Before the referendum, voters were asked to choose whether the UK should 'Remain a member of the European Union' or 'Leave the European Union' (McCann, 2016). However, many subsequent questions and interpretations show the ambiguity of the chosen words – Remain and Leave. People interpreted each word differently and now, with hindsight, it appears that if there was another referendum, the outcome may be different. This observation suggests that the tool used (the content of the schedule) was not highly reliable because the consequences of the choices had not been itemized.

Planning your research

1 Research focus

- Think about the discipline your research falls under. Is it a single field of study or multidisciplinary? – for example, humanities, business and finance, social science and health, etc.
- What is your research interest? – for example, human resource management, organizational behaviour, innovation and entrepreneurship, accounting, banking and finance, etc.
- Narrowing it down further – what is your research title?

2 Undertaking a literature review

- Acquaint yourself with the available online databases related to the discipline.
- Search for related literature on the subject.
- Make a list of the literature available for this topic.
- Who are the key authors in this field?
- What are the major debates on the subject?
- What are the gaps in the literature?
- What are the existing models or frameworks?
- Are there any areas of further research or development?
- Will a new or different methodology lead to new knowledge?

3 Formulating your research questions

- What is your main research question? Avoid questions that require a 'yes' or 'no' response.
- Are there any sub-questions requiring answers?
- What research philosophy applies to your research questions?
- What data is required to answer your research questions?
- What is the appropriate research method – e.g. qualitative, quantitative or mixed methods – to use?
- What are the appropriate data-collection instruments?
- Are you developing a new instrument?
- Are you choosing an already established valid and reliable instrument?

4 Creating a data-collection plan

- What is your unit of analysis? – i.e. the entity that you are trying to analyse. Who or what are they?
- Where will you collect your data?
- Who will you collect data from?
- What are the data-collection methods available for this study?
- Which data-collection method is more appropriate?
- Are you proficient in the use of the specific method you plan to adopt?

- What training will you require to further improve your knowledge of research methods and data analysis?
- How will you demonstrate the reliability and validity of your data and research instruments?
- Have you considered triangulation? – i.e. ensuring credibility by using multiple approaches or data sources to analyse your data.

5 Selecting research participants

- Do you know the population?
- What is your sample size?
- If you are adopting a quantitative method, is the sample size representative of the population? Is it precise?
- How will you select the sample size? For quantitative analysis, consider using sample size calculator software available online.
- How will you identify or recruit the participants?
- Is it a cross-sectional study (different people at one point in time) or longitudinal study (same sample at separate points in time)?
- What are the ethical considerations you need to be aware of?

6 Fieldwork/collecting data from research participants

- Have you explained why you are requesting their participation? – you will need to inform them that their participation is voluntary and that they can decline or withdraw at any point in time?
- Have you given them the background to the study?
- Have you explained why and how you have selected them?
- Have you explained the rationale for your research? Why is the study necessary?
- Have you briefed them on what to expect? – for example, the forms they will be required to complete and how long the interview or survey will last.
- Have you clarified the research purpose – i.e. academic?
- Have you given them the assurance that their information will be confidential and reported as anonymous, depending on the situation?
- Have you clarified what you will do with the information and how the data will be stored?
- Have you checked if they have any questions regarding your request?

7 Ensuring data integrity

- How will you keep the information you have collected intact and accurate during your study?
- How will you secure the information to prevent unauthorized access?
- How will you back up your data?

- How will you authenticate your data to ensure the reliability and validity of the collection process and during the analysis?
- Which reliability and validity measures will you use? Why are the selected measures appropriate?

8 Data analysis

- Do you have the requisite skills for data analysis?
- What are the data-collection methods appropriate for this analysis?
- How will you determine the statistical significance?
- How will you record your data?
- How will you present your data?
- How will you ensure the validity and reliability of your data?

9 Resources required

- Have you considered the duration of the course and how much time you have?
- How will you fund your study?
- Who would you look to for support and be accountable to for your progress?
- How would you manage family and personal commitments?
- What training would you require to help you build confidence in research methods and academic writing?

Chapter 4: summary

In this chapter, the author has explained that a PhD is a postgraduate academic degree granted to successful students on the submission of a thesis (or dissertation) within a higher educational institution's stipulated guidelines. At all times, the end product of the research must result in an original contribution to knowledge. The author has suggested practical steps that would help researchers produce new research worthy of earning this prestigious academic degree.

Chapter 5 considers the relevant research skills you will find useful on your academic journey. These include learning how to avoid plagiarism, managing time, making an effective PowerPoint presentation and knowing about the benefit of joining a Research Interest Group, which entails learning from others' experiences of the research process.

5   Research skills required

By the end of this chapter, you will be able to:

1 Avoid plagiarism
2 Identify the types of plagiarism
3 List some plagiarism detection tools that you could use
4 Identify the top Time Thieves
5 Apply self-management techniques to deal with Time Thieves
6 Plan your schedule to meet deadlines
7 Present your research effectively using PowerPoint

Plagiarism – the assassin that terrorizes the world of academia

Universities have ways to keep the unwelcome assassin at bay – but many students have faced expulsion because they plagiarized. Certainly, the UK has installed powerful technology to identify any evidence of plagiarism in scripts. All students, from whatever part of the world, need to be fully aware that electronic screening will easily identify and expose strains of plagiarized content. So, what then is plagiarism and how can you identify it?

Definitions of plagiarism

> Plagiarism is the act of stealing someone else's work and attempting to 'pass it off' as your own. This can apply to anything, from term papers to photographs to songs, even ideas! (Lowe, n.d.)

Cardiff Metropolitan University, for example, provides a clear example of the assassin:

Plagiarism can be defined as using, without acknowledgement, another person's words or ideas and submitting them for assessment as though it were one's own work, for instance by copying, translating from one language to another or unacknowledged paraphrasing (Cardiff Metropolitan University, 2019, p.2).

So, to avoid plagiarism you must:

1 Use quotation marks when you copy verbatim and ensure you cite properly.
2 Acknowledge the original author in the text and include them in the references when you paraphrase another person's idea, text, figure or diagram.
3 Not employ the services of essay banks or other agencies to write your work.
4 Not use unacknowledged content from the internet.
5 Not reuse your own material (previous submission) in your thesis except when you have been granted permission by the department.

(Cardiff Metropolitan University, 2019, p.2)

Types of plagiarism – further examples

Lowe (n.d.) listed four types of plagiarism. These include:

1 Copying

This is where a student copies word for word (verbatim). An example of this would be if you took some else's assignment and submitted it as your own by replacing the author's name with your name. Another example would be if you lifted a text from a source word for word and omitted quotation marks and the appropriate in-text referencing for the copied text.

Example of copying

Let us take an extract from my unpublished paper, K.S. Iornem (2020b). 'International students' perspectives on surviving a PhD in the United Kingdom: navigating the emotional and academic journey', and then illustrate the difference between a correct citation and copying. The correct procedure:

It must be mentioned that a number of doctoral students attributed some of the study challenges, in part, to lack of support from their supervisors. Hence, supervisors and universities need to recognize that international students face many difficulties, ranging from adjusting to a new environment and culture to learning independently. Furthermore, pastoral care should rest not only with the supervisors but the PhD programme administrators as well. (Iornem, 2020, p.5)

This is correct because the verbatim passage is put in quotation marks, or indented if the quote is long – usually more than a few lines – and placed in a separate paragraph, as in this example. The author is cited and the page number included.

The incorrect procedure – plagiarism (copying)

It must be mentioned that a number of doctoral students attributed some of the study challenges, in part, to lack of support from their supervisors. Hence, supervisors and universities need to recognize that international students face many difficulties, ranging from adjusting to a new environment and culture to learning independently. Furthermore, pastoral care should rest not only with the supervisors but the PhD programme administrators as well.

Problem: no acknowledgement of the author. The impression is that the words and ideas are all yours. However, with Turnitin or other plagiarism software checkers the assassin will be exposed! Even if the author was cited, but the copied text was not put in quotation marks or indented, you will be presenting the impression that you paraphrased the text – and this is plagiarism.

2 Patchwork plagiarism

Patchwork plagiarism is another of the assassin's disguises and is similar to copying. Here, the plagiarizer changes some words in the original text or adds new ones without putting quotation marks around the copied text, or indenting it. To illustrate patchwork plagiarism, consider the same extract (the plain text is copied and the bold words are the paraphrased words):

*It must be **noted** that **several PhD** students **ascribed** some of the study challenges, in part, to lack of support from their **professors**. Hence, supervisors and universities need to recognize that international students face many difficulties, ranging from adjusting to a new environment and culture to **studying** independently. **Consequently, counselling** should rest not only with the supervisors but the **head of the department too**.*

If we had put the copied phrases in quotation marks and added a citation after the quotation, like (Iornem, 2020b, p.5), we would have been safe from plagiarism. For example:

According to Iornem (2020), several PhD students ascribed some of the study challenges, in part, to lack of support from their professors. 'Hence, supervisors and universities need to recognize that international students face many difficulties, ranging from adjusting to a new environment and culture to [studying] independently' (Iornem, 2020, p.5). Consequently, counselling should rest not only with the supervisors but the heads of the departments too.

3 Paraphrasing plagiarism

Lowe (n.d.) explains that summarizing someone's work (in your own words) without acknowledging the author or source is yet another mask that the assassin wears, and it is wrong. Using synonyms, and changing some words but keeping the ideas and sentence structure without acknowledging the source, does not change the reality that plagiarism is present.

Example of paraphrasing plagiarism (using the same extract from Iornem, 2020b)

Research suggests that supportive supervisors help students to progress on their academic journey and this contributes to the students' timely completion of the doctoral programme. Therefore, stakeholders like supervisors and PhD programme administrators need to empathize more with international students on a new journey trying to adapt to the culture and legislation of their host country and university.

Here, the whole passage has been completely rewritten, but the idea remains the same, and the author is not acknowledged. This is nothing less than stealing. Remember that examiners are experienced, trained and alert to the presence of the assassin – no matter in what disguise.

4 Unintentional plagiarism

Unintentional plagiarism is another notorious disguise of the assassin.

1 Incorrectly citing a source: this occurs when you cite the wrong source unknowingly. For example, sometimes an author writes about research that someone else has done, but you are unable to track down the original document. In this case, instead of including the source you did consult in your references, you include the primary source-giving the impression that you consulted the original material. I have seen many students do this, sometimes unintentionally.

2 Also, some students plagiarize because they do not know about the different types of plagiarism. For example, in the case of the copying example (without the quotation marks), even though the author has been acknowledged, the lack of quotation marks (or indent for long quotes) gives the impression that the work was paraphrased, when it was actually copied verbatim. This is also an example of unintentional plagiarism, assuming the student was unaware.

3 Using another person's work incorrectly. For example, if you misrepresent an author or change the entire meaning of his or her work, and then cite them as the originator – when in fact you have given a completely different interpretation of their work. Dishonest use of an author's work is considered as plagiarism (Lowe, n.d.).

Although you may have committed plagiarism unintentionally, you will still be penalized. It is similar to the legal principle that says, 'ignorance of the law is no excuse'.

Avoiding plagiarism

Lowe (n.d.) explains some simple ways of avoiding plagiarism:

1 You should be honest. The quality of your research is dependent on the quality of your sources and the critical review of your paper. Therefore, where you have used a source, acknowledge the author of the original work cited.

2 As much as possible, you should create your own content. Using others' works excessively can be interpreted as plagiarism.

3 Ensure you quote and cite your sources correctly.

4 If you are in doubt as to whether to cite or not, then by all means cite. It is, at least, safer.

How universities detect and report suspected plagiarism

1 Plagiarism checkers highlight similarities in submitted work and help students and assessors to determine what aspects of the work is owned by the student.

2 Plagiarism detection software has helped to curb academic misconduct, especially as students are made aware of the consequences.

3 The software guides assessors to quoted and paraphrased content, and reveals the sources from which the texts are copied. Furthermore, plagiarism detection tools have empowered students to reflect and improve on their academic skills and take ownership of their work (www. turnitin.com).

4 Cardiff Metropolitan University's Unfair Practice Procedure requires that cases of plagiarism be reported to the Academic Registry. They supply the lecturer/examiner with the relevant forms to complete, as documentary evidence must be provided – for example, extracts of the student's work highlighting the plagiarized content, along with information on the source(s). The university advises against solely using the plagiarism detection software statistics (e.g. Turnitin) as the only measure of determining academic misconduct. They recommend that an interpretation of the results be offered in establishing the plagiarized content (Cardiff Metropolitan University, 2019, p.6).

Plagiarism software checkers

Turnitin and iThenticate are among the most common plagiarism detection services, and to access their helpful features you need to pay an annual subscription/licence fee. Many publishers, government organizations, non-profit and other professional organizations use iThenticate to verify originality. Turnitin is 'the largest provider of monitoring software to British universities' (Yorke, 2018).

There is also free software available. Pappas (2013) lists the top ten free plagiarism detection tools that you may care to explore:

1 Dupli Checker
2 Copyleaks
3 PaperRater
4 Plagiarisma
5 Plagiarism Checker
6 Plagium

7 PlagScan
8 PlagTracker
9 Quetext
10 Viper

Pappas also provides more information about the advantages and disadvantages of each tool at https://elearningindustry.com/top-10-free-plagiarism-detection-tools-for-teachers.

Other free plagiarism detection tools include Copyscape and Grammarly (you can pay for an upgrade to receive a fuller service).

Ensuring consistency in referencing

The examples and references in this book follow the Harvard referencing system. However, even within Harvard style there are variations between universities – for example, in the guides to Harvard referencing by Anglia Ruskin University (2019), the University of Exeter Business School (2014), and the University of Leeds (n.d.).

Some common inconsistencies students often create are due to using variations of referencing style in the same document. Note the following examples:

1 'Hackman **&** Oldham (1974)' – 'Hackman **and** Oldham (1974)'
   Note the variations '**&**' and '**and**'.
2 Also, when quoting directly – note the page number style:
   Oshagbemi (2003:**364**) research found that there is a 'strong positive relationship . . . between pay satisfaction and gender'.

   Oshagbemi (2003, **p.364**) research found that there is a 'strong positive relationship . . . between pay satisfaction and gender'.
3 In the reference list – note the volume and issue number:
   Wright, T.A. and Bonett, D.G., (2007). Job Satisfaction and Psychological Well-Being as Nonadditive Predictors of Workplace Turnover. *Journal of Management*, **33(2), p.141**.

   Wright, T.A. and Bonett, D.G., (2007). Job Satisfaction and Psychological Well-Being as Nonadditive Predictors of Workplace Turnover. *Journal of Management*, **Vol 33, no. 2, p.141**.
4 Also note another variation – the year without brackets and single quotation marks for the article title:
   Wright, T.A. and Bonett, D.G., **2007**, 'Job Satisfaction and Psychological Well-Being as Nonadditive Predictors of Workplace Turnover', *Journal of Management*, 33(2), p.141.

Action point: The key is to maintain a consistent referencing style throughout your work.

Different referencing styles

As academics, we will continue to make scholarly contributions in different jurisdictions. It is therefore important to acquaint ourselves with other referencing styles in different countries. There are around a thousand different styles, including APA (American Psychological Association), MLA (Modern Language Association), Oxford, Chicago, Vancouver, and so on.

Information about the respective styles can be found online. This information is important so you are able to distinguish between the styles used by authors in different countries and to be able to tell if papers are properly cited or not. Also, remember that as you progress up the academic ladder you may be involved in supervising students from other countries that adopt different referencing styles. Therefore, it is vital for you to have knowledge of the preferred style a particular institution adopts so you can guide the student accordingly.

Dealing with Time Thieves – suggested success tips

'There is a time for everything, and a season for every activity under the heavens' (Ecclesiastes 3:1)

Do we not all struggle to meet deadlines? Do we find ourselves unwilling losers against the ever-ticking clock? Haven't we read books on effective time management to 'get organized'? Over the years, writers have generated debates, shared their opinions and earned money from those of us who read their books – because we want to manage time and remain disciplined about keeping within time-bonded settings. However, as is argued, time cannot be controlled because it is set, and so it cannot be managed (Jones and Loftus, 2009; Taylor, 2018)! However, there is one thing we can control – ourselves. Hence, it is preferable to refer to it as 'self-management' rather than time management. Our challenge on the PhD journey is how to manage/organize ourselves within the time frame of our three to five years of full-time study – depending on the university.

Top eight Time Thieves to avoid

Here are some suggestions on the top eight Time Thieves to avoid.

Personal disorganization

Looking for a pen, car keys, or trying to retrieve files on our computer can be so frustrating – and time-wasting! For example:

1 As a writer, I often have handwritten manuscripts on my table, some of which I have not converted to electronic copies. I have had situations where my wife cleaned the house and threw away pieces of papers with my notes.

2 There have been times when my daughters entered my study to get a piece of paper to do their writing, and unwittingly took important manuscripts.

3 There were situations where I was typing an important document and left it for a while. My daughter came to play with my computer and pressed the keyboard, adding text which distorted my document.

To avoid these problems:

1 Give people limited access to your work space, or keep your essential documents out of sight and save yourself the trouble of having to rewrite all over again.

2 Have a proper filing and organized system.

3 Have a place for your stationery.

4 Have a particular style for saving your files on your computer. For example, when you modify a specific document you can safely store it by adding V2 (version 2), V3 (version 3), and so on to the file name. That way, you will be able to retrieve the latest modification.

5 Save documents in different places. Imagine you finished typing your thesis and the file 'disappears'! I witnessed a PhD student crying because her computer crashed, and she lost her over 70,000-word thesis. I asked why she did not back up her work on a USB stick, to which she replied, 'I did, but I can't find my flash drive.' Her work of over two years was gone, and I can only imagine how devastated she felt. Sometimes the little things we take for granted can cost us dearly. I recall typing the Preface for this book when, without warning, my computer rebooted. As I could not recover what I had typed, I painfully rewrote it.

So please:

• Save the file to your computer.
• Save the file to a USB.
• Email the file to yourself.
• Always save in multiple files and email copies of your work to yourself.

Multitasking

We often find ourselves doing many different things at the same time. In most cases, this happens because we are not able to distinguish between what is important and what is urgent.

1 Covey's (2004) 'four-quadrant time management system' suggests that when a task is important and urgent, you do it immediately. The important and urgent quadrant includes – crisis, pressing issues, deadlines and some meetings.

2 When a task is important but not urgent, you decide when to do it. The important and not urgent quadrant includes – preparation, planning, relationship building, forming strategies and personal development.

3 When a task is urgent and not important, you delegate. The urgent and not important quadrant includes – some emails, interruptions and some meetings.

4 When a task is neither important nor urgent, you dump it. The not urgent and not important quadrant includes – excessive TV/games, some phone calls and wasting time on social media.

5 Always give yourself a deadline of one to two weeks before the given deadline. Then work to your own deadline. This strategy worked effectively for me.

Distractions and interruptions

The arrival of visitors, an influx of emails and repeated phone calls cause us to forget essential activities. However, if we do not plan our day (as with Covey's four-quadrant system), we will be swamped (not in the positive sense) doing other people's tasks or engaging in that which is unimportant. Learn to say 'NO' to some of the 'NOW' requests.

1 A to-do list can be helpful – a systems management tool. For example, setting reminders on our computer or mobile phone. My systems management alerted me about filing my annual returns one week in advance, then three days before, then one day before, and on the D-day itself. My systems management worked.

2 Use a Gantt chart – one of the most widely used tools for project planning. It gives a visual view of the tasks planned over a given period, and is a useful way of showing what task/activity is scheduled to be done on a specific day. With a Gantt chart you can see the start and end dates of a project from one simple viewpoint (ProjectManager, n.d.).

Gantt charts help you to schedule when (month/year) you would complete tasks such as:

- writing chapters
- preparing data-collection instruments
- data collection and data entry
- data analysis and interpretation of results
- findings and discussions
- conclusions and recommendations
- preparing draft reports
- the final report and submission.

3 The Pareto 80/20 rule is helpful in enabling us to focus 80 per cent of our time and energy on the 20 per cent of work that really matters.

4 Another way to achieve this is by having a defined key result area (KRA). 'A key result area is defined as something for which you are completely responsible. This means that if you don't do it, it doesn't get done. A key result area is an activity that is under your control' (Turla, 2006). When people approach us to do a task for them, Turla (2006) suggests that we ask ourselves, 'Is what I am about to do going to contribute to my KRA?' If it does not, then we refuse and

explain the importance of the tasks at hand and how their request will affect our KRA. Again, this method helped me achieve a lot on my PhD journey.

5 Develop a template for answers to frequently asked questions. That way when we receive an influx of emails we can respond immediately without having to write each response from scratch.

6 We may also wish to incorporate time in our planning to accommodate disruptions – for instance, planning time for family, planning time for work, planning time for other extracurricular activities.

System failure

Desktops, laptops, projectors and any electronic system you use in your work are subject to technical problems. These can be time-consuming and frustrating, so here are some suggestions for managing technology.

1 Is your computer system updated and is antivirus software installed?

2 Do you shut down your PC/laptop when not in use for a lengthy period – say, ten hours?

3 If we proactively allow time for unexpected technical problems, we should face less stress. For example, when delivering a PowerPoint presentation why not assign ten minutes for sudden system failure – in other words, make sure that you sort your computer or, if the computer is for public use, go there ahead of time to check that all is in order before your presentation.

Poor communication

'The meaning of your communication is the response you get . . . while your intention may be clear to you, it is the other person's interpretation and response that reflects your effectiveness' (Rist, 2016). Poor communication could also be in the form of lousy handwriting, when others are unable to read it. Students sometimes fail to communicate effectively – for example, failing to explain to their supervisor (albeit unintentionally) why he or she was unable to attend an appointment. In some cases, it might be the result of a psychological barrier, such as a personal problem affecting their academic progress. We also saw in Anna's story (Chapter 1) that her supervisor was incommunicado for about nine months. When he eventually became available, he made Anna start her research afresh because she was heading in the wrong direction. Anna's supervisor failed to communicate the reasons for his absence, and this demotivated her.

Here are some suggestions for improving communication:

1 Bazrafkan et al. (2016) recommend that you meet with your supervisor regularly to discuss your research and ways you can improve on your coping skills, critical thinking and problem-solving methods. This can help you to overcome stress and anxiety on your PhD journey.

2 Always make sure one or two trusted people proofread your work. That way, if they have problems understanding any part of it they will ask to you

explain or rewrite it. My proofreader was very good at this. He would include a comment for me to rewrite if he did not understand a passage. He would also ask me to provide examples to make the meaning clearer. This exercise can save you a great deal of time before your final submission.

3   You need to get feedback when giving verbal instructions, so that the message is clear. For example, ask the individual to summarize your instructions – that way you can correct them if they have not clearly understood. Remember the acronym KISS – Keep It Short and Simple.

4   Always use correct grammar and punctuation.

Meetings

Meetings without a defined agenda eat up precious time. These suggestions will help to maximize time at meetings.

1   The convener of the meeting must communicate the agenda to members ahead of time (at least 48 hours before the planned meeting) to enable educated preparation. The convener could also request input to augment the planned deliberations.

2   Stand-up meetings are often better than seated sessions because, in most situations, it will cut out unnecessary waffle – especially from those who love the sound of their own voice!

3   When putting out the notice for a meeting, inform members that it will start promptly. Appeal to participants to come on time and make sure everyone stays within the time slot they have been assigned to speak. Ensure that meetings do not go way beyond the scheduled finish time. For example, if you intended a meeting to end by 2 pm, you should not go beyond 2.20 pm, otherwise this may discourage participants from joining discussions early since your meetings end late.

Procrastination

People procrastinate because they are avoiding unpleasant or difficult tasks. For some, it is the fear of making a mistake, while for others it is a habit (Jones and Loftus, 2009). On your PhD journey there will be many demanding tasks that you will be tempted to put off to a later date, but please avoid procrastination.

1   Consider Mark Twain's advice about procrastination. He likened it to eating a frog. 'The first rule of frog eating is this: if you have to eat two frogs, eat the ugliest one first . . . The second rule of frog eating is this: if you have to eat a live frog at all, it doesn't pay to sit and look at it for very long' (cited in Tracy, 2017). This is the crux of procrastination – pushing difficult tasks to a later date.

2   You may also wish to consider your personal prime time – i.e. when you are most active. For some, it is in the mornings, while for others it is in the afternoons or evenings. It is advisable to carry out these 'procrastination prone' tasks during your prime time. My personal prime time is in the early hours of the morning – say, from 6 am. I am able to make meaningful progress during this time. This is probably because I will have had enough sleep, and feel refreshed.

Beware of plagiarisers

During my transfer interview, I had to submit the first four draft chapters for the interview process. The examiners were pleased with the quality of my work, and they passed me without corrections. One examiner said it was the best work she had come across that day. I was excited and shared my experience with my colleagues. Then two of my friends asked to see my work so they could follow my pattern. Of course, I shared it with them because I thought my work was already saved in Turnitin (the plagiarism software checker).

Surprisingly, another student due for the transfer interview had heard how well I performed. He wanted me to proofread his work and make suggestions. When I was going through his work, I noticed his methodology chapter was similar to what I had written. When I confronted him, he said he received my work from one of the friends I had given a copy of my draft chapters to. I had to report this to the programme leader, and he asked me to give him the names of those I had shared my work with. He said if they submitted their work before me, I would be accused of plagiarism. The programme leader then advised that I should never give a soft copy of my work to anyone other than people I trusted. Subsequently, I had other people ask for soft copies of my draft chapters, but I refused. Some of them began to make comments that would make me feel as though I was selfish and did not want to help colleagues. It did not bother me because this was my journey and I had committed so much money and time to the work, so I would not allow an individual to cause me to fail. But time was used up having several meetings with the PhD programme leader about the issue, and my research stood still in the process.

Join a Research Interest Group

What is a Research Interest Group (RIG)?

'A Research Interest Group is a cluster of faculty, researchers and PhD students working on a common research theme. These groups evolve over time and represent emerging areas of research strength in the school' (Loughborough University, n.d.).

The aim of Research Interest Groups

The idea behind the establishment of Research Interest Groups is to stimulate discussion, research and publications through the collaboration of supervisors, directors of studies and students working in related academic areas. Each RIG normally has a chair who exercises leadership and coordinates a programme of meetings and other activities. RIGs normally formulate the specific titles that reflect the collective interests of the group (Harper, 2015).

Benefits of a Research Interest Group

The University of Glasgow (n.d.) highlights the opportunities which a RIG will offer:

1   To find out about research activity in the department.
2   To learn from other's experience in conducting research.
3   To explore and address methodological challenges.
4   To gain an international perspective of your discipline from colleagues.
5   To participate in practical workshops.
6   To increase confidence in discussing your research.

The importance of a RIG cannot be overemphasized. It is like a therapy session where you go to meet like-minded people to hear about their problems and how they have been able to address them. You get the necessary support to help you overcome your challenges. You receive feedback on the progress you have made so far and recommendations on how you can make your work better. So by the time you are ready for your viva you will have benefitted from a variety of perspectives, and this will lead to increased confidence when you are defending your thesis. Groups are open to staff and postgraduate research students in the department who have an interest in conducting research. You can check with your PhD programme leader to find out more about RIGs and how you can get involved.

Presenting your research using PowerPoint

While doing your PhD, you will be required to attend academic seminars. You also have to present your research to other students and some faculty members at your university. This process is usually to get feedback and suggestions on how to improve your research.

I recall my PowerPoint experience as a first-year PhD student. I shared my draft PowerPoint slides with my supervisor for his feedback. My supervisor explained that too much text would result in my audience reading the slide before I spoke, thus removing the element of surprise and causing many to become bored. He advised that I needed to use key phrases and bullet points, and then expand on each. I found his feedback helpful.
Here is my example:

- Slide 1 – my title and name
- Slide 2 – background and thesis argumentation
- Slide 3 – aims and objectives
- Slide 4 – a partial listing of theories that influenced my study
- Slide 5 – my conceptual framework
- Slide 6 – my research methodology
- Slide 7 – the potential contribution to knowledge
- Slide 8 – summary and conclusion.

Interestingly, I was commended by the faculty because the texts were legible, and I was able to elaborate on my bullet points. I used large font sizes – 48 for headings and 36 for the body of each slide. I also made sure the text colour contrasted significantly with the background colour – for instance, I used black text on a white background. After my presentation, many of the students requested a copy of my presentation and began to follow my style.

An effective presentation depends on your PowerPoint slides. In one of the British Academy of Management Conferences I chaired, many students made similar mistakes of preparing wordy slides with backgrounds that made them difficult to read. For example, one student used black text on a dark-green background. Furthermore, just like my supervisor had said, we could read the entire wordy slides before the student had finished reading them, and then there was nothing new for the student to say. Another difficulty was the font size and style. The student had used small font sizes – my guess would be 24 for the body and 30 for the headings.

So, with PowerPoint slides, I would recommend that you:

- Stick to one theme font – for example, Ariel, Calibri or Times Roman.
- Avoid too much text on the slides. The simpler, the better, so KEEP IT SHORT and SIMPLE (KISS).

Figure 3 Preferred

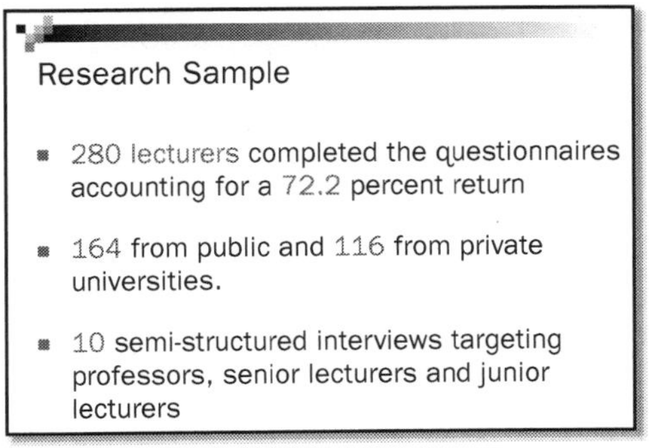

Research Sample

- 280 lecturers completed the questionnaires accounting for a 72.2 percent return
- 164 from public and 116 from private universities.
- 10 semi-structured interviews targeting professors, senior lecturers and junior lecturers

Figure 4 Avoid (too much text)

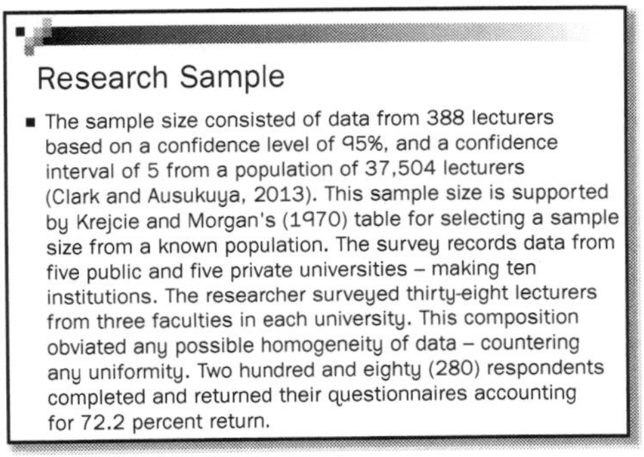

Research Sample

- The sample size consisted of data from 388 lecturers based on a confidence level of 95%, and a confidence interval of 5 from a population of 37,504 lecturers (Clark and Ausukuya, 2013). This sample size is supported by Krejcie and Morgan's (1970) table for selecting a sample size from a known population. The survey records data from five public and five private universities – making ten institutions. The researcher surveyed thirty-eight lecturers from three faculties in each university. This composition obviated any possible homogeneity of data – countering any uniformity. Two hundred and eighty (280) respondents completed and returned their questionnaires accounting for 72.2 percent return.

Figure 5 Readable

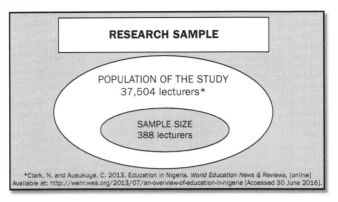

Figure 6 Avoid (unreadable – text blends with background)

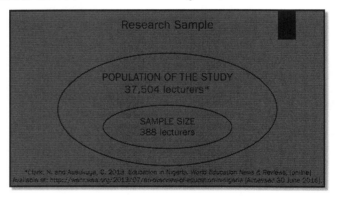

- Use at least a 48-point heading and a 36-point font size for the body.
- Ensure there is a high contrast between the text and the background.

Chapter 5: summary

The author provided steps on how to avoid plagiarism. He identified the top Time Thieves and suggested practical self-management techniques to help you meet your scheduled deadlines. For example, there is information about how to make an effective PowerPoint presentation to ensure you leave a positive impression on your audience – the dos and don'ts have been itemized to increase your skills as a presenter.

Chapter 6 addresses the problems of style and structure that often confront students when they begin the thesis-writing process. The chapter provides guidance on thesis structure and chapter-by-chapter word count requirements, as well as a guide for drafting an abstract, along with examples.

6 Structure of a good PhD thesis

By the end of this chapter, you will be able to:

1 Create a good structure for your thesis
2 Use the rule of thumb for each chapter word count
3 Recognize the importance of the thesis argument

PhD thesis word count – a guide

Higher education institutions have different word count guidelines for PhDs. In the UK, a PhD thesis in social sciences, arts and humanities is not expected to exceed 80,000 words, *excluding* the bibliography, but including the table of contents, tables, footnotes and appendices (University of Cambridge, n.d.; University of Leicester, n.d. b). For some universities, it is expected to be over 50,000 words (for example, University of Leicester, n.d. b), while for others it should be more than 60,000 words (for example, Cardiff Metropolitan University, 2018).

There is, however, a consensus among UK universities that a PhD thesis should normally not exceed 100,000 words, including the bibliography, tables, tables of contents, footnotes and appendices. If you want to exceed the word limit, you will need approval from your institution's Research Degree Committee, but I strongly advise you to refrain from going over the prescribed word limit: 'A dissertation that exceeds the limit may not be examined until its length complies with the prescribed limit' (University of Cambridge, n.d.).

Thesis structure

Your PhD thesis could follow this format:

- Chapter 1: Introduction
- Chapter 2: Literature Review
- Chapter 3: Conceptual Framework

- Chapter 4: Methodology
- Chapter 5: Data Analysis
- Chapter 6: Discussion
- Chapter 7: Conclusion and Further Discussion

(Patel, 2015, p.8)

Check with your supervisor and the university's guidelines for the recommended thesis structure as this also varies from institution to institution. Some universities accept 5 chapters; others may accept 5 to 11 chapters. The onus is on the student to check what is accepted by the university. Remember, only include what is necessary.

Word count for each chapter

We have established that an ideal PhD thesis in social sciences, arts and humanities will normally be between 70,000 to 100,000 words. Therefore, as a guide, Shahedi (2015) suggests that the rule of thumb for each chapter may be as follows:

1 Introduction: 5 per cent of total words (from 3,500 to 5,000 words).
2 Literature Review and Conceptual Framework: 30 per cent of total words (from 21,000 to 30,000 words).
3 Methodology: 20 per cent of total words (from 14,000 to 20,000 words).
4 Data Analysis: 25 per cent of total words (from 17,500 to 25,000 words).
5 Discussion: 15 per cent of total words (from 10,500 to 15,000 words).
6 Conclusion and Further Discussion: 5 per cent of total words (from 3,500 to 5,000 words).

Important points to remember

1 Quality is better than quantity – a good PhD thesis should explicitly help the reader understand the objectives, the research puzzle, the significance, the theoretical foundation, methodology, results, analysis and discussion of the results and recommendations.
2 Put yourself in the shoes of the reviewers who read your thesis. 'Be direct and to the point . . . do not forget, it's not what you write, it's what people need and read' (Apsimon, 2013).
3 The value of your thesis lies in your novelty/originality. Ensure the specific contributions to knowledge are clearly articulated.
4 Do not get hung up on trying to use vocabulary that is 'out of the ken' of the average reader. Use academic English, but refrain from using so-called 'intellectual' wording to impress readers.

Thesis argumentation

According to Patel (2015), the first step to writing your PhD is using the 3S approach, which he describes as Story, Structure and Sentences:

1 **Story:** What's your story? Where did you get the concept?
2 **Structure:** When you have answered the first question, the next questions are: How do you structure it? How do you organize it? What should come first, and what should follow?
3 **Sentences:** Having pictured and thought about your story, how do you begin to write. How do you write sentences that will connect with the reader?
4 Start with the thesis argumentation in the opening paragraph.

The importance of the thesis argumentation (opening statement) is that the:

1 opening sentence locates the thesis – for example, 'This thesis argues . . .'
2 opening paragraph takes you to the work – for example, 'This is because current theory is deficient in . . .'

You can use connecting sentences to link each preceding chapter to show your argument in each of the seven chapters.

Questioning articles

Patel (2015) advises that early career researchers should learn to question articles they consult. They should achieve this by seeking answers to the following questions for each article they review:

- What is the argument/logic?
- What is the methodology?
- What is the interpretation?
- What is the assumption?
- What is the contribution?
- What is the conclusion?

Figure 7 3S approach to thesis writing

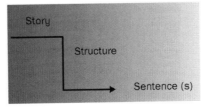

Patel (2015, p.8)

Other useful tips

1 At the end of your research, you ought to have achieved your objectives or answered your research question(s). The conclusion should show how you have achieved each objective.

2 Thesis paragraphs should be about ten lines long. Avoid too many short paragraphs.

3 If you can, ensure each chapter has its own table of contents. This helps examiners to see the chapter contents (again). The table of contents page for each chapter should be printed on coloured paper to make it easy for examiners to open new chapters. Remember that a thesis of about 70,000 to 100,000 words is voluminous, and examiners often take breaks in between. Therefore, using this style shows consideration for your examiners.

4 Make sure you have an introduction and a summary for every chapter.

5 Always have an outline for each chapter or section. An outline helps you to structure your ideas in a logical fashion. It also guides you on what is important and helps you to stay focused and search for relevant resources based on the content in the outline. Jot down points, and then you can expand on them properly when you begin to write.

6 Consult as many literature sources as possible then filter and select the contents for your work (especially credible sources).

7 Never include any information that you are unable to explain. I learnt this lesson while writing my undergraduate dissertation. I had quoted an author and was unable to explain the relevance of the quote when my supervisor asked. He then advised me never to include any information I could not defend.

Figure 8 Writing up your thesis

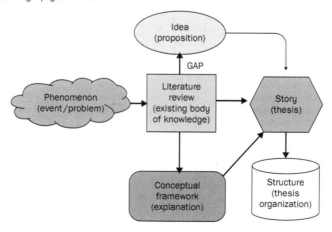

Patel (2015, p.8)

Writing an abstract

An abstract is written after you have completed your thesis. It is a 150- to 300-word summary of your thesis. The abstract should inform readers of the key aspects of your work: what you did, how you did it, your findings, and the implications of your findings. As simple as it may look, the abstract is one of the sections that must be spot on because it is the door to your thesis. Remember the principle of Ockham's razor – the simpler, the better. Never add anything that could be left out. And, as always, remember that different institutions have different requirements.

Saeidi (2016) provides a guide for drafting an abstract:

1 The abstract should be a single paragraph and should have a block format – that is, the first line should not be indented.
2 The purpose of an abstract is to provide a brief and comprehensive summary of the study.
3 It should be accurate – do not include information here that is not in the body of the manuscript.
4 It should be self-contained – spell out abbreviations.
5 It should be concise – 150 to 300 words, depending on the university.
6 It is a good idea to write the abstract last.
7 Start the section after the abstract on a new page.
8 Avoid citing references in the abstract.
9 Use the active rather than passive voice – but without personal pronouns.
10 Use the past tense for procedures and the present tense for results.
11 The content of the abstract of an empirical study is:
   a The problem under investigation – in one sentence, if possible.
   b Information about the participants of the study, including their age, sex, ethnic and/or racial group, and proficiency level.
   c The essential features of the method of the study, including instrument, treatment, and so on.
   d The basic findings, including effect sizes and confidence intervals and/or statistical significance levels.
   e The conclusions and implications of the study.

Example of an abstract

Extract from 'International students' perspectives on surviving a PhD in the United Kingdom: navigating the emotional and academic journey'.

Abstract

The doctorate is quite an emotional undertaking filled with dilemmas and frustrating dead-ends. However, despite the vast research on how to achieve a successful PhD, there seems to be little in its content that empathises with international students who, on their academic journey, seek to navigate and adapt to the culture and legislation of their host country and university. This study examined several challenges faced by international students undertaking a doctoral degree at universities in the United Kingdom. Seventeen participants comprising ten final-year PhD students and seven recent PhD graduates were interviewed over the period of four months. A thematic analysis of the interviews revealed that: (1) most students residing in the UK with their families took longer to complete the doctorate, which was due to them balancing study time with working long hours in order to meet their families' financial needs; (2) immigration restrictions accounted for an astounding 80% of the emotional distress experienced by PhD students, often leading to either prolonged years of study or academic withdrawal; (3) having a supervisor who supported students as well as empathised with them accounted for around 90% of the overall academic success and subsequent graduation. It is hoped that the second finding emerging from the study will encourage the UK Visas and Immigration (UKVI) division of the Home Office to debate a visa policy that meets the needs of doctoral students and is separate from a Tier 4 (General) student visa. A full-time PhD takes between three and four years to complete, depending on the academic institution. With that in mind, it would be of great benefit to grant, for instance, a five-year (PhD) student visa, thus bringing the much needed reassurance in course completion at doctorate level, and promoting the continuing, supportive and all-inclusive nature of the host country (Iornem, K.S. 2020).

Chapter 6: summary

Chapter 6 recommended a thesis structure and gave advice about chapter-by-chapter word counts for students to use as a guide, and also explained how to use fewer words to describe your thesis to ensure better understanding of the content.

The next chapter explains the importance of publishing in peer-reviewed journals during your PhD journey. This proactive step will give you a better chance of submitting well-researched work with a greater possibility of success at the viva stage.

7 Doing a PhD: why it is important to publish

By the end of this chapter, you will be able to:

1 Appreciate the importance of publishing
2 Adapt your PhD to each publication's requirements
3 Make an informed choice about whether to remain in the field of academia or find other employment

Publishing your research

I recommend that you publish your research in a peer-reviewed journal during your PhD studies. I have listed the benefits below. However, in many instances, because of the revisions required by the peer reviewers, it may take several months before your article is accepted.

Check the requirements of your university. If publishing is a must, you have no choice but to ensure you follow their conditions. However, even if publishing in a peer-reviewed journal is not a mandatory requirement of your university, I recommend that you make an effort to get your work published. Notwithstanding, please pay attention to time limits and other relevant factors (immigration status, money, personal responsibilities – just to mention a few) that can delay your graduation.

There are other considerations as well. For example, during my studies, I deliberately did not publish because it was not mandatory at my university. Also, I had minimal time because I was working part time, studying full time, and also raising a young family. Furthermore, at my university, students were required to complete many forms if they published part of their thesis. This was intended to address the high level of plagiarism resulting from part of a student's published thesis. I considered this procedure time-consuming and did not want to increase the plagiarism risk.

However, immediately after passing my viva I submitted my research to the editors at the British Academy of Management, and after I had satisfied the peer reviewers my paper was accepted for presentation at its 2018 annual conference. After that, it was published in the *Journal of Higher Education Theory and*

Practice (Iornem, 2018). The next sections buttress the importance of publishing, offering advice on adhering to the guidelines required by journal editors, and the pros and cons of going into full-time academia or seeking other employment.

The importance of publishing

A PhD is a research degree, and the knowledge generated by any doctoral research contributes to the academic and professional development of society. Prominent among the theories affirming the importance of published research is the new growth theory. The concept emphasizes that knowledge and innovation are major drivers of modern culture (Ruttan, 1998). In corroborating this view, Inekwe (2015) asserted that research is the critical determinant of economic development. The importance of publishing research outcomes cannot be overemphasized.

Apart from contributing to societal growth, publishing has other benefits for the doctoral student. First, PhD training at most universities around the world (including the UK) requires doctoral students to 'publish or perish' (Postgrad. com, n.d.). This suggests that publishing several papers can be legally essential for a Doctor of Philosophy degree. Furthermore, the process of publishing helps doctoral students to develop the vital skills needed to succeed in their graduate school. According to Lawson and Smith (1996), writing skills are refined during the publication process – the scholar learns from the constructive feedback provided by reviewers. And Brownlow (1997) says that having a manuscript published is also evidence of a student's ability to understand data collection and analysis – skills that graduate schools expect from every doctoral student.

Furthermore, publishing creates many opportunities. It brings attention and recognition to researchers/scholars and their institutions. With an increasing number of academics competing for funding, the quality and quantity of publications may invite funding opportunities. Universities, among other organizations, often use the number of published papers credited to an individual to measure his or her competency. As lecturing jobs within the education sector continue to be more competitive, the number of publications is widely used as criteria during the recruitment process. Thus, it is not enough for doctoral students to simply do well in their coursework. Those who want to secure postdoctoral fellowship or teaching jobs must make themselves stand out through publications. This suggests that those who publish infrequently may find themselves out of contention for many teaching job opportunities. It is for these reasons that there is an increasing need to publish.

Publishing your research results is essential for growth in academia and career progression. If research outcomes/results are not published, other scholars cannot see and appreciate the value of the knowledge/evidence generated – neither can they build on it further. It is through research and findings that academia's influence grows.

Adapting to each publication's requirements

Doctoral students are encouraged to publish one or more first-authored research works before their graduation because their school relies on these to strengthen the institution's position for every funding opportunity. According to Li et al. (2015), getting your paper published as a PhD student can feel overwhelming as you may have to learn about the publication requirements and processes. However, this problem can be avoided by knowing and following the journal's instructions for writers when preparing a manuscript. With a quick internet search, a student can learn the specific requirements essential for publication.

Generally, there are several publication requirements that every author should follow. The specifications detail how a manuscript for submission to a peer-reviewed journal should be prepared. These are usually available on the journal's website, and include:

1 Title
2 Abstract
3 Introduction
4 Theoretical background and hypotheses
5 Research methods
6 Discussion
7 Conclusion
8 References
9 Appendices

(Green and Johnson, 2006)

Adapting to these requirements is a prerequisite for accepting submitted manuscripts. Thus, when formatting a paper for publication, doctoral students, along with other scholars, must observe these instructions before submission.

Other specific requirements include ensuring the manuscript adheres to the recommended reference style (American Psychological Association, 2010). Pay proper attention to details such as in-text citations and spacing requirements provided by the journal editors. By checking for appropriate use of grammar, spelling and punctuation, you can improve the quality of the manuscript submitted, and this will likely reduce the number of revisions cited by reviewers.

Considering career options: academia or other employment?

The choice of whether to remain in academia or find other employment is a primary concern of most doctoral students. You will need to consider the opportunities available in academia. For example, think about your continued interest in research and then weigh it against other careers. In my personal circumstance, as a management practitioner and lecturer, I aim to publish research related to my core competence – management practice. This then increases the number of my publications that will be useful should I choose to pursue a full-time lecturing career.

In this section, I review the advantages and disadvantages of contemporary industrial and academic career paths for doctoral graduates. Remaining in academia to pursue the traditional route of becoming a professor is the default decision of most postgraduate students. While many career advisers often encourage doctoral students to take this path, observations have shown that obtaining a successful academic career is increasingly difficult. This, according to Martin Shepperd, Professor of Software Technologies and Modelling at Brunel University, is due primarily to the increasing numbers of doctoral graduates and the limited number of universities willing to hire fresh doctoral graduates (cited in Marten, 2015). In spite of this, deciding to remain in an academic environment has several advantages.

One significant advantage of working in an academic setting is the work flexibility it offers. Except for the time you might spend in teaching and a few other administrative tasks, you usually decide how to dedicate your hours to different responsibilities, and you can plan your holidays. This is in contrast with the industrial setting where most employers would expect you to conform to fixed working schedules (Sauermann and Roach, 2016). In addition to the above, being in an environment full of people with great minds helps you to develop a sense of pride that feeds your decision to make it to the professorship level and get involved in student mentorship (Cyranoski et al., 2011).

Apart from working in academia, the other option available to a doctoral student is to find employment in an industrial setting. Job opportunities for doctoral graduates in commerce and industry may range from research and development (R&D) positions, to management and production positions that may require fewer research skills. In the case of R&D positions, one could still experience the intellectual freedom of academia, but usually in a restricted manner. In a management/production position, there is no room to use the research capabilities developed during doctoral training, even though the doctoral degree may still translate to a higher entry level and salary. In summary, the advantages of finding employment in an industrial setting include higher remuneration, the feeling of immediate real-world impact, and probably a better work–life balance (Sauermann and Roach, 2016).

Regardless of the above, there is also a higher chance of losing the benefits (intellectual freedom, work flexibility and involvement in mentorship) associated with academic positions. Thus, even if your target is to find other employment, a short-time job in academia after your doctoral programme is an option to consider as it could enhance your chances of getting full-time R&D jobs in industry. The skills in presenting ideas, writing scientific papers or supervising students can be advantageous for your career, even if it is not in academia. Therefore, remaining in the field of academia or finding employment in the marketplace has both advantages and disadvantages. It is crucial that every doctoral student, before graduation, considers both options rather than settling straight for an academic position by default. So, be aware of the opportunities and risks and make an informed career path choice.

Chapter 7: summary

If you are considering a lecturing job after your PhD, then it is essential to note that many higher education institutions insist that their faculty members publish several academic papers. This is equally important for your reputation as an academic, and most promotions at universities are also based on the number of a lecturer's publications.

The next chapter will help you understand that a PhD journey of three to five years can be tiring and complicated. The author, therefore, shares his experience and the avenues you could explore to help sustain you on your journey.

8 How to keep yourself motivated

By the end of this chapter, you will be able to:

1 Identify the sources of motivation for your research journey
2 Avoid communication barriers with your supervisory team
3 Learn how to manage/organize yourself within the time frame of your research

Introduction

You are embarking on a journey that will take about three to five years to search for and acquire new knowledge.

Remember that:

1 You have a time frame and deadlines to achieve your objectives.
2 You have a limited budget.
3 You have to live up to a strict code of conduct, and ethical considerations set out by your university.
4 You have your own personal challenges.
5 You have various stakeholders' options to consider.

Furthermore, the key ingredient to starting and finishing your PhD is motivation. My experience underscores the reality that this top degree requires determination energized by rooted motivation.

My motivation found its roots in:

1 My supervisory team
2 My dad
3 My proofreader
4 My colleague
5 My family

6 My peers also studying for a PhD
7 My career vision

My supervisory team

My supervisor was very supportive. Unlike the experiences of many peers, my supervisor was a star.

1 Throughout my PhD, he attended all my seminar presentations.
2 He was at my confirmation interview.
3 He conducted a mock interview with me before my mock viva.
4 He was at my final viva voce.
5 He provided all the support I needed.
6 He was available to sign forms.
7 Consequently, this amazing individual was someone I never wanted to disappoint and take for granted.

Remember, supervisors are very busy people, so try and keep to agreed appointments and deadlines. For example, my supervisor usually arranged his programme to meet with both of his students – myself and another a PhD colleague. He would give an appointment time of, say, 11 am for the first student and 12 noon for the second (i.e. a one-hour meeting for the first student and another one hour for the second). Imagine if he was to meet us at the scheduled times and one of us did not show up – he could have sat there for close to an hour until the allotted time was up.

Your PhD is a going to be a three to five-year journey. As noted, different reasons – immigration status, personal, money, supervisor relationship, and so on – can mean students sometimes go beyond the study duration. A good supervisor–student relationship is crucial to the progress you will make on your academic journey. Students (including myself), who make fantastic progress on the PhD programme, confess that the supervisor's professional guidance is a key contributing factor. Similarly, an unhealthy relationship has implications. In Chapter 1, three PhD students (Anna, Fazil and Esi) suggested that their supervisors were among the reasons for their prolonged time on the programme.

Let's revisit the experience of each student:

- Anna's supervisor was not always around. He was incommunicado for about nine months. When he eventually became available, he made Anna start her research afresh because she was heading in the wrong direction. Although her supervisor supported her with materials and useful feedback, the problem was the time it took the supervisor to respond because of his busy schedule.
- Fazil stated that his first challenge on the PhD programme was not academic but supervision. He said he became depressed because he did not receive the professional support he had expected from his supervisory team. He later

changed his supervisors. This time he got a supervisor who was very supportive, and his research expertise made Fazil progress quickly.

- Esi also complained that she did not get along with her new supervisor. Esi had to put up with her, but faced even more problems. She wished she had changed this second supervisor from the beginning. Esi said her colleague who changed her supervisor was able to complete her PhD within four years, having got the necessary support from her new supervisor.

Bazrafkan et al. (2016) suggest you talk regularly with your supervisor about any problems and discuss ways you can improve your coping skills, critical thinking and problem-solving methods. My advice is, if the issues persist, please consult your academic programme leader for assistance. The programme leader may assess the situation and advise on an alternative course of action.

My dad

Being the financer of my PhD, and as an academic, my father was interested in my research. Interestingly we retain similar interests, so it was easy to get the necessary resources and advice on how to overcome some of the challenges I came across. He shared ideas on how to address many conundrums and always emphasized the importance of keeping a positive working relationship with my supervisor.

My proofreader

My proofreader was a trusted friend, a mentor and an English-language tutor and lecturer in business and related academic subjects. His pro bono offer enabled me to complete my academic journey. He was the motivator who contacted me when I had not sent him sections of my work. He also took an interest in my research, my family and my progress. We worked as a team and discussed any recommendations that, at the end of the day, I would accept or reject because the thesis was my work.

My colleague

As a happily married man with two daughters, I always had to balance and prioritize my responsibilities as a student, working part time, and as a responsible family man with a supportive wife.

My colleague Siona and I began to discuss our research journey together. Siona was single and had her priorities – different to mine – but was nevertheless progressing at a faster rate than me (even though I started my PhD journey before her). I started working closely with her and keyed into her determination to achieve her three-year goal. Because she was now ahead of me in her work, she unconsciously became my mentor. She helped me by sharing how she overcame her challenges to achieve her set objectives, and disclosed how she smoothed out her administrative challenges. Siona shared feedback from her mock and then final viva, thus enabling me to avoid many of the pitfalls of a PhD journey. I made it a point of duty to follow her 'bumper to bumper'. For example, whenever she submitted a document, I would endeavour to do the same within a week. When she submitted her thesis for the mock viva, I also tried to work on outstanding sections and submit mine as well, and, one month after her viva, it was my turn! Her mock and final viva experiences made it easier for me to defend my thesis because of her guidance and expertise in facing the examiners.

Siona and I graduated at the same ceremony – I was the only student to graduate from my cohort at the 2017 ceremony. I then became a motivator for fellow PhD peers and started providing advice based on my experience and, so far, two of them are preparing their final submissions for their vivas.

Please note that different people have different motivations to achieve their goals. For example, Siona did not want to pay extra fees for extending her programme as that would be way outside of her budget – the cost element was a major factor. This reminds me of my days as an undergraduate. I studied metallurgical engineering at Ahmadu Bello University, Zaria, Nigeria, and this was a five-year course. However, because of strikes leading to school closures, my studies were extended to seven years. But when the university management increased the tuition fee from NGN 5,000 to NGN 17,500 per semester, I decided to take all my courses at once to avoid paying an extra charge for another semester and I graduated in six years. Lack of funds can serve as an excellent motivator to help you achieve your goals within your stipulated budget.

My PhD friends at other universities

I had friends at other universities who were also studying for their PhD. We often checked up on each other to find out how we were progressing. Whenever either of us achieved a milestone in our research, we would call to share our excitement. This was a positive reinforcement – especially as each of my friends graduated before me. I attended some graduation ceremonies, and that gave me a sense of assurance that my day was going to come as well.

My family

Sometimes you have family members who are very proud of you and your achievements and you do not want to let them down. You read and hear how they speak highly of you, and you are obligated to live up to their expectations. My immediate family – my wife and daughters – waited expectantly for my graduation, and we shared warm and strengthening times together.

My professional capacity

I organize capacity building courses for executives and individuals interested in career development. Before commencing my PhD, when I spoke at leadership seminars, often during my presentations, delegates would refer to me as 'Dr Shadrach' or 'Prof Shadrach'. It made me uncomfortable having to correct them and say that I had not attained that academic level – yet! Once you are working in education and training, some people expect you to have achieved a PhD. Others consider you highly placed in academia once you have got a PhD. So, somehow, the titles 'Dr Shadrach' and 'Prof Shadrach' also contributed to achieving my desire to earn a PhD.

Chapter 8: summary

The author has identified sources of motivation to help you on your research journey. He has explained how you can avoid communication barriers with your supervisory team and has shared his experience on how he organized himself within the time frame of his research.

Chapter 9 highlights the importance of having an excellent proofreader and the action points you should take note of to produce a well-written paper-free of grammatical errors.

9 Proofreading and editing

By the end of this chapter, you will be able to:

1 Appreciate the value of a good proofreader and editor
2 Adherence to the rules required for thesis, when these are in conflict with some formal English writing rules
3 Recognize the importance of submitting your thesis chapter by chapter for proofreading and editorial feedback

Find a professional proofreader

You will need a good proofreader on your PhD journey. However, proofreading is expensive so be cautious when choosing someone. Do not try to cut corners by using someone who would make you redo your entire work. Employ a professional proofreader – an individual who carries a recommendation – to work with you. I was fortunate to have a proofreader who was also an English-language teacher. He provided chapter-by-chapter proofreading and editorial comment on my thesis, and happily agreed to do this on a pro bono basis. However, there were instances where we disagreed on grammar and structure.

I have shared some of my stories here, along with suggested action points to help you:

1 As a teacher of English language, he did not seem to like a specific thesis style of writing that was not in consonance with or violated English language rules. For example, while my supervisor advised that each paragraph in my thesis should be at least ten lines, my proofreader disagreed. He argued that paragraphs could comprise less than ten lines. However, in this case, we agreed to stick to what my university supervisor wanted – after all, he was going to assess my work. Remember, academics differ in their opinions – English grammar is crammed with exceptions to the rules – respect the differences and aim for your degree.

Action point

Remember to stick to the thesis rules when they conflict with some formal English writing rules.

2 Remember that the thesis is your work. The final responsibility for its content is yours. Therefore, work with your proofreader who, like you, is an imperfect human. Always check what has been proofread, and if you note instances where errors still exist, contact your proofreader immediately so that they are aware of any slip ups. In my case, out of respect for his heavy schedule, I sent him my work chapter by chapter so that he had more time to focus on my thesis. I noticed that this method helped him (and me). So, respect your proofreader's schedule and be responsible for submitting your work at the agreed time – he/she is not a robot.

3 My proofreader often asked me to rephrase sections of my work because the content was incomprehensible. You see, I was in too much of a hurry and wanted to meet a word count before sending it to my supervisor. My proofreader's suggestion to rephrase the content was most helpful and was emphasized by my university supervisor who explained that there will be many iterations as well as possible rearrangement of text between chapters, so there is no need to get hung up about sectional word counts, or even the overall word count. He encouraged me to send drafts, or individual sections, so that we could see the thought processes and the evolution, rather than a big bang end product.

Action point

Give your proofreader enough time to go through your work. The more work you give, the more time you should provide. Different proofreaders require different time limits – dependent also on the context of the work. A chapter-by-chapter approach is sensible and courteous and will help the proofreader understand the flow and direction of your thesis. Remember that your relationship with your proofreader is essential – be humble, open-minded and prepared to learn!

4 Another issue was that my proofreader was strict with the academic style of writing that, in some cases, requires the use of synonyms to replace words that are similar in meaning. However, some academic topics have unique terms for a technical definition, so if you use synonyms you may change the meaning. For example, while proofreading my 'research methodology' chapter, he changed 'research method' to 'research approach' because I had used 'method' in the earlier paragraph. But in research methodology, 'approach' and 'methods' are not synonymous. 'Research methods' refer to either quantitative data from surveys, qualitative data from interviews and observations, or mixed methods – a combination of both qualitative and quantitative methods. On the other hand, the 'research approach' refers to whether you have adopted deductive, inductive or abductive reasoning – the three primary research approaches.

So, as you can see, synonyms cannot be used in all cases. However, it is helpful to let your proofreader know why you disagree. Happily, my proofreader readily complied with my reasoned objections to his suggested changes and always encouraged me to make my own decisions throughout. He, like me, remains a willing learner.

Action point

You can always override your proofreader's suggestions where you have evidence that you are making a specific or technical point supporting your argument.

My proofreader was very thorough. He addressed formatting issues, made suggestions and provided valuable feedback. Whenever he completed proofreading any material that I sent to him, he would send it for my approval and ask to go through the final version again. This made my work very tidy, and led my supervisor to remark 'You seem to have a particularly good proofreader.'

Chapter 9: summary

This chapter explained the importance of having a proficient proofreader and editor. The author suggested steps you should take if the thesis rules conflict with some formal English writing rules. He highly recommended submitting your material chapter by chapter for proofreading and editorial feedback.

You are probably getting closer to completing your thesis and looking forward to sitting your mock or final viva. Chapter 10 provides guidance on how supervisors recommend external examiners to the head of the research committee, and explains what examiners want to see in a thesis. The author has also shared his experience of meeting a difficult examiner and has highlighted some dos and don'ts to help you achieve a successful viva outcome.

10 Handling changes recommended by supervisors and examiners

By the end of this chapter, you will be able to:

1 Appreciate the relevance of feedback from your supervisors and examiners
2 Learn ways to address recommended changes to your study
3 Avoid the pitfalls of perfectionism

Supervisors and examiners want you to pass, but . . .

One of the challenges many students face, having gone 'too far' in their work, is knowing how to respond to being asked by their supervisors to make some major changes. For example, you may be asked to collect new information after you have already finished your data analysis. Or, it could involve making an addition that is going to affect your work significantly, thereby extending the time you might be required to spend on the programme.

I have witnessed many students engage in serious disagreements with their supervisors or mock viva examiners. The mock viva is defined as an oral exam which you sit in preparation for the final viva. In other words, it is the test you undertake before the live oral exam. In structure, it follows the same approach as the live exam: once you have been assessed, you receive feedback on how well you have done, changes you need to make and an evaluation of whether your work would merit a PhD or not. After the mock oral exam, you will be required to reflect constructively on the feedback and address the examiners' concerns. As part of the process, you may be given an indication of the length of time you have to make the corrections.

Before I proceed, I would like to reassure you that your supervisors and examiners have your best academic interests in mind. This is the notion you must keep in mind, so as to be able to accept, and respond efficiently to, the changes or amendments they are proposing.

In addition to acting in your best interests, supervisors also have a reputation to protect. Firstly, your supervisor might be present on the day of your viva along with their peers. Now, let us hypothesize that your work has been poorly laid out. In such a situation, the examiners might be falsely led to assume that your supervisor was to blame for 'allowing' you to showcase such work. You can only imagine how embarrassed the supervisor would feel if you lacked confidence to defend what you have been working on for a few years!

Secondly, your work might be available online, for everyone to access, and if it does not meet the expected standards this could tarnish the supervisor's reputation. Examples of work that might receive negative criticism can range from using a wrong or inappropriate research method, to failing to consider relevant theories that ought to influence your study, or even grammatical and punctuation errors left unedited in written presentations.

I believe you can now better understand and appreciate why supervisors often encourage you to make changes to your draft before the final submission. Notwithstanding, there are some students who remain worried when supervisors recommend the introduction of new concepts or amendments, as they are sceptical about the feasibility of such additions.

Saving time on corrections

I would love to discuss perfectionism at this stage. I would have introduced it in the section on 'Dealing with Time Thieves', but, instead, I have decided to cast a spotlight on it in this section because it fits perfectly with the theme. By perfectionism I mean aspiring to present your research perfectly in every way. In other words, dotting the i's and crossing the t's. Broadly speaking, this is a very good approach – but when it comes to research, let me 'burst your bubble', so to speak. Although I am very much tempted to say 'there is no such thing as perfect research', I absolutely must point out that there is always room for improvement and, as such, you will always receive suggestions on how to better your work from your supervisors, other scholars and examiners. Perfectionism can be a huge time-waster, with consequences. Let me demonstrate this with an example of two students sitting a paper in an exam hall. As the clock shows the final minute of the exam has approached, the invigilator signals that the time is up and asks the candidates to submit their scripts. The first student, though able to complete only about 60 per cent of the questions, hands in his paper straight after hearing 'time is up'. The second student, who has completed at least 80 per cent of the exam, but feels there is more to do, continues to write despite the invigilator's announcement. That student may risk being penalized and his paper may not be accepted because he failed to heed the instructions. By implication, the student who submitted 60 per cent of his work would be better placed than the one who, having completed 80 per cent of the script, had his paper rejected for failing to adhere to the exam conditions. The same would happen if you were expected to submit your assignment on a designated academic portal at a given date and time. Failure to submit at the stipulated time leads to a penalty. Therefore, when you are time-bound, perfectionism can potentially lead to grave consequences.

I have observed many students striving for perfect research, spending more years on it than perhaps necessary. Aspiring to perfect your research is excellent – but do note that, as you are investing more time, sometimes even years, new research is also unfolding. When you get to the viva stage, an examiner might ask, for example, whether you have taken into consideration the ground-breaking work by Kohol Iornem in your research! My comment on perfectionism notwithstanding, I want to reiterate that quality research requires quality time. Therefore, as much as possible, make sure you spend enough time producing work of very high standard – meaning fewer mistakes requiring fewer corrections.

Another way to deal with proposed changes to your research is to consider them as a limitation to your study and therefore including this in the section on 'Limitations to the study'. I would like to caution here that the changes I am referring to are those which you can justify to the satisfaction of your supervisors and examiners. One way to look at this is to ask yourself these questions: 'Will my work in its current form merit a PhD?'; 'Have they explained the relevance of the recommended changes and how it would improve the quality of my study?'; 'Will my research process and outcome be undermined if I fail to make the necessary changes?' I would suggest that you consider revisiting Chapter 4, 'What is a PhD?', and Chapter 6, 'Structure of a good PhD thesis', to see how you can demonstrate to your supervisors and examiners the quality of your research.

Worthy of note is that people are different. They have different approaches to research. In some instances, when you do not follow their style and cannot justify why they should accept your approach, they will make suggestions for you to consider. So my advice is to always take on board the corrections and input from your supervisors. Make the recommended changes and show them how and where the corrections have been made. Where you cannot make a change, explain to your supervisors and examiners why this is so. They may accept your explanation as long as it does not significantly affect the outcome or quality of your research.

Dealing with amendments – my story

I would like to share my experience of how I handled suggestions for amendments. After I had collected data for my research and analysis, I prepared a paper which I presented at an academic conference. During the presentation, one of the conference chairs recommended that I include an analysis of culture and its impact. This was a very good suggestion that would have contributed significantly to new knowledge. However, the problem was that I had not collected any data on culture. Taking on board the given suggestion would have meant needing to design another questionnaire and travel to Nigeria to collect data. This was, in my mind, practically impossible considering the time left before my final viva, the project logistics and travel costs I would incur.

Besides, as I believed at the time, the initial data I had already collected helped me to achieve my objectives and, therefore, my research was 'good to go'.

So, what did I do with the conference chair's comment instead? I took it on board and included it in the section on 'Recommendations for further research'. By doing so, I was in a position to demonstrate to the examiners my awareness of the suggested contribution to knowledge and, at the same time, I justified why I was unable to carry out the advised analysis in my paper.

Thinking back to my final viva, I can still recall those moments when the internal examiner would occasionally ask, 'In our closed-door meeting earlier, you said you were not happy with this aspect of his research. Do you have any further questions for him?' – to which the external assessor would simply respond, 'He has already addressed it in his explanation.'

So, in the end, I passed. I had only minor corrections to make before achieving the desired result. I was simply asked to include the explanations I had given during the interview. Most focused on justifying why I had used the Mann–Whitney U Test, the reasoning behind the theories at the core of my analysis, explaining their strengths and weaknesses, and revisiting my conceptual framework in light of the findings (because some factors were later merged into my final analysis). It took me only two weeks to make all the amendments. I merely created subtitles within relevant chapters of my thesis and then included the suggested changes, which were mostly justifications.

Chapter 10: summary

Being sincere in your studies is an essential requirement of the PhD process. By this I mean letting people know what you have worked on, how you did it, why you did it, where you did it, what you found, and who will benefit from it. Furthermore, it can be insightful to share the good, the bad and the ugly of your research – i.e. to let other scholars know what you have experienced.

I cannot emphasize enough the importance of this section on handling changes recommended by supervisors and examiners. This is the stage where many students probably get within arm's reach of the finish line, yet the feedback from supervisors or examiners can still demoralize them. However, I want you to remember, once again, that most supervisors have your best interests in mind but, at the same time, have a duty to protect their own reputation and that of their institution.

The next chapter provides a guide to appointing an external examiner. The chapter also suggests ways to ensure your examiners enjoy reading your thesis. You will learn useful tips on how to handle difficult examiners and how to prepare for your viva.

11 Mock viva and viva voce preparation

By the end of this chapter, you will be able to:

1 Follow the author's guide for appointing an external examiner
2 Make it easier for the examiner to plough through your work
3 Meet the requirements that examiners look out for in a thesis
4 Learn useful strategies for dealing with difficult examiners
5 Apply the dos and don'ts for achieving a successful viva outcome

Appointing an external examiner

Appointment of an external examiner is the stage immediately after you have finished your mock viva (and corrections, if any). This milestone indicates that you are finally on your way to completing your PhD journey. However, you can experience difficulties, which can lead to further delays. As a result, I have suggested tips in line with my experiences along with my supervisory team. I hope these snippets will be of help to you.

1 Before your supervisor suggests an appropriate external examiner, it would be helpful if you could write down a set of keywords which best describe your thesis, and what specific area of expertise you would require your examiner to have. This information will help your supervisor decide on a choice. Provide your supervisor with your list of six to eight keywords.

2 The recruitment process takes at least a few weeks. Also, some of the academics your supervisory team prefer may already be busy with other commitments. Remember, you are one of many in the queue.

3 Your supervisor will start by asking for CVs. The Research Degree Committee can advise you of the rules for engaging external examiners and the likely timescales to appoint one before organizing the viva.

4 Your supervisor will need to look at the profiles of research academics (e.g. publications, PhD student supervision experience, and so on). Senior lecturers

with a strong publication history, readers and professors (who are research-focused) in your general area, would be acceptable. It may take some time to locate an appropriate individual. As already mentioned in point 2, academics are very busy (with teaching, administrative duties, meeting attendance, completing research projects/articles/books to tight deadlines). You need to give those your supervisor has contacted a fair chance to reply. It would be reasonable to give them a week or ten days to respond.

Make it easy for the examiner to read your hard work

A typical PhD thesis word limit varies between subjects and is usually shorter for science-related disciplines. However, for social sciences, arts and humanities it can range from 70,000 to 100,000 words. Reading the content must be enjoyable – like taking a walk in the park! Therefore, I have suggested ways in which you could achieve this.

Include an introduction and a summary for each chapter

Include an introduction at the beginning and a summary at the end of every chapter because it is easy for examiners (and you!) to always reflect on what they have just read and the content that will follow. Furthermore, you will find that you may work on various chapters at different times. So, to make sure you connect your topic and also link to your readers, explain what you will write about at the beginning and then end with a summary – plus a peek into the next chapter. Think of the opening section as the diving board from which the reader can gain an overall insight into what they will dive into. Consider the ending as shaking off the water from the pool and leaving the drops as evidence of what you have just written, and then add a tiny glimpse into the next chapter as well.

Chapter introduction

Pat Thomson, a professor of education at the University of Nottingham, suggests helpful strategies for connecting chapter to chapter introductions. This simplified approach aims to address the 'getting lost' problem and proposes a good way to keep yourself as the writer, and the reader, on track. Though the author refers to it as a 'link–focus–overview' approach, I prefer to describe it as 'link–focus–link'. I have demonstrated how a chapter introduction would look (using the contents of Chapter 2 of this book as an example):

First paragraph – the link

You should LINK the new chapter by referring to the preceding chapter. In other words, summarize the last chapter in the opening sentence. For example, '*Chapter 1 noted that PhD candidates can learn from the ups and downs of other PhD graduates and how they overcame their hurdles. The chapter also highlighted the practical challenges faced by many PhD students from across the globe.'*

Second paragraph – the focus

FOCUS by highlighting the content of the new chapter and its relevance. You should justify how the content connects with the overall study. For example, *'To better contextualize the study, this chapter explains some of the fears students express when embarking on a PhD journey. This information is important because . . .'*

Third paragraph – the link

Now that the reader understands the FOCUS, it is important they get a glimpse of what will follow in the next chapter. For example, *'The next chapter, Chapter 3, discusses the entry requirements, which include having a master's degree, showing evidence of competency in the English language and submitting a personal statement and research proposal about your intended field of study . . .'*

Chapter conclusion and summary

What should the conclusion cover? This should be a brief summary of the most critical points in the chapter. It is like saying to the reader, if you do not remember anything at all from what you have read in this chapter, these are the essential points - and then list them. Thomson (2014) expects authors to have these questions at the back of their mind when drafting the chapter summary:

1 What do you want the reader to remember about this chapter?
2 What is the key to the argument you have made – the most significant thing(s) that they have to keep in their mind as they go forward?

Thomson (2014) further explains that a conclusion should be short and to the point. She contends that when you get to the concluding chapter, it's crucial you return to the FOCUS on what you wrote in the beginning – in other words, what did you set out to achieve? According to the author, it helps you to check what you proposed to cover in the chapter from the onset and then compare it with what you have actually covered. Then you should ask yourself if you have achieved this? If you have not included your fundamental concepts, you can revisit the chapter to amend the arguments accordingly and then reconsider the chapter summary and possibly the introduction to ensure that there is a consistent and logical flow.

Table of contents for each chapter

After the mock viva, one of the examiners advised me to create a table of contents for each chapter (alongside the original table of contents). She also suggested that the first pages of each chapter have a different paper colour (for a bound thesis). According to her, examiners sometimes start looking at your work and take breaks in between, so the coloured pages make it easier to open a specific chapter.

Remember, when you make it easier for the examiner to plough through your work, this could affect their mood and edge them to be more positive. Of course, examiners have different styles, but I am sure this style would be appealing to many. However, I must emphasize that before you adopt any style, check and abide by your university's recommended structure.

What examiners look out for in a thesis

During your viva voce examination there will be more than one examiner. In most viva examinations there is a chairperson, who moderates the exercise, and a minimum of two assessors – the internal and external examiners – who liaise on the outcome after the exam. Please remember that each examiner holds different expectations and requirements. Nonetheless, a consensus will be required to decide on the acceptance of your thesis. I have made use of information from ten examiners' comments on students' theses during the viva voce (oral examination). The information below is not exhaustive and is intended to serve as a guide for your final preparations before submitting your thesis for assessment.

1 **Examiners will seek to understand what your thesis is about**

    Each will check to see if your topic, abstract, aim, objectives and research questions are in consonance.
    - Does your topic contain the relevant variables?
    - Is the content appropriately phrased, thus confirming the thesis objective(s)?
    - Have you ensured that the thesis title reflects the content?

2 **Examiners will verify that each chapter has an introduction and summary**

    If every chapter begins with an introduction, it will be easier for the examiner to read and understand. The opening tells the reader about the chapter contents, and the summary recaps the critical issues addressed in the chapter and then links to the next chapter. Ensure that you structure the thesis chapters logically.

3 **Examiners will check for grammatical/typographical errors throughout the thesis**

    Your writing style along with correct use of grammar is the easiest way for examiners to understand your argument and invoke their interest. As far as possible, use the services of a proofreader or friend. Furthermore, it is ideal to revise your work at different times and focus on content improvement throughout – for example, consider focusing on the style, clarity of meaning, concepts and grammar.

4 **Examiners will analyse whether you have clearly expressed the strengths and weaknesses of the theories that influenced your research and the rationale for their inclusion in your work**

If you have developed a model, they will check to see if you have explained how the model can be used as a contribution to practice. Make sure that your literature review accurately reflects the fundamental theories underpinning the topic and justify their inclusion in the content.

5 **Examiners will check to see that you have elaborated fully on the link(s) between the nature of the data and the decision to use a specific instrument for your data analysis**

- Have you justified your purpose, role, methods and methodology and the acceptable reasons why you did not consider the alternatives?
- Have you ensured that the methodology chapter introduces the tensions, concerns and decisions associated with the research topic?
- Remember to give details of how the questionnaire strategy was navigated in practice and the decisions made on sample size regarding saturation.

6 **Examiners check to see whether you have revisited the discussion, conclusions and recommendations and considered and reflected on and made any possible amendments in the light of the current research findings**

Have you clearly showed the focus of the thesis and considered the recommendation that may be explored in further work?

7 **Examiners check to see that the specific contributions to knowledge are clearly articulated in the study**

You will need to make clear the contribution to knowledge the thesis makes by providing the evidential basis of the input and its generalizability into the broader research context. You should consider reviewing the pertinent literature by constructing a summary table. Such a table should make it easier to detail the literature gaps. The justification rendered for conducting research should be based on past literature and the gaps therein. Therefore, the key literature needs to be effectively presented.

8 **Examiners check the formatting throughout your thesis to ensure consistency (for example, single space for indented quotes, 1.5 or double line spacing for body text, in line with your university's requirements)**

This could be your thesis structure, referencing or font styles. You can use past students' theses from your university as a guide. Universities normally have samples of completed students' theses/dissertations which you can use as a guide for the conventional structure and format.

9 **Examiners check to see if you have sorted the referencing – page numbers/quotation marks consistently**

For example, during my mock viva the examiner asked why I had the names of three authors mentioned in the in-text citation in some places and in others I had written 'et al.'. I explained that the format of the Harvard reference style I used was to list all three authors, but to use 'et al.' for more than three, and I made sure this was consistent throughout my thesis. Another point that was made was about the page numbers in my reference list. I had the pages in the references written as 'pp.', even for single pages, but she corrected me and explained that when you have a single page you designate it as 'p.' and multiple pages as 'pp.'.

Note the 'pp.' in multiple page numbers and 'p.' in the single page number:

Ssesanga, K. and Garrett, R.M. 2005. Job satisfaction of university academics: perspectives from Uganda. *Higher Education*, 50(1), **pp**.33–56.

Tett, R.P. and Meyer, J.P. 1993. Job satisfaction, organisational commitment, turnover intention, and turnover: path analyses based on meta-analytical findings. *Personnel Psychology*, 46(2), **p**.259.

I would advise you to spend a great deal of time addressing any inconsistencies in your reference list before your final submission. It is the simplest way for examiners to see if your thesis will be easy to follow, or something they will dread looking at.

Also, many people make the mistake of using the first name in their citation. Often this is unintentional, because of the conventions of the first name and last name. For example, some people may write 'IORNEM, Kohol' while others may write 'Kohol Iornem'. So, if you are not careful, you might use 'Kohol' as the last name, as in the former example. For instance, during my mock viva the examiner noted that I had an in-text reference 'Peter (2014) cited in . . .'. She suggested that 'Peter' was an unlikely surname, and asked if I had meant 'Peters'. Unfortunately, I had used a secondary source that cited the work as 'Peter (2014)', so we then had to check my secondary source to get the full reference information. We then searched for the reference on Google, and lo and behold the author's name was Peter Mason. So, the correct in-text citation was supposed to be 'Mason (2014) cited in . . .' and not 'Peter (2014)'.

Since that experience, I have had a chance to check other students' dissertations and have picked up on similar errors. The examiner picked this up because she was aware of standard English surnames. The correct format which the author should have written is:

Mason, P. 2014. *Researching Tourism, Leisure and Hospitality for Your Dissertation*. Oxford: Goodfellow Publishers Limited.

not

Peter, M. 2014. *Researching Tourism, Leisure and Hospitality for Your Dissertation*. Oxford: Goodfellow Publishers Limited.

This is the disadvantage of relying on secondary sources. The author you are quoting may have used the wrong name – as we have just noted or may even misrepresent the original author's idea. It is important that you also look up the secondary source, read it to understand the argument/idea, and cite directly. Don't rely solely on secondary sources.

10 Examiners check to see if you have cited recent publications and articles from high-impact journals

It is crucial for you to consider using publications from renowned peer-reviewed journals. Peer-reviewed journals use the 'double-blind' peer-review policy. Here, two reviewers – researchers with an interest in the related discipline – review your work and provide unbiased feedback on how you can improve it to merit publication. There is no guarantee that, because it has undergone a double-blind review, the quality will be high. Therefore, consider using journals with a high-impact factor. The impact factor is a measure of a journal's importance. It shows how frequently journal articles are cited. With the help of the impact factor, you can compare journals within specific (but similar) fields. The impact factor is calculated as the total number of citations for all articles published in the preceding two years, divided by the total number of articles published in those two years (UCL Institute of Education, 2018). While the impact factor suggests the quality and relevance of journals, it is not without criticism. For example, if articles in a journal are referred to many times in the same journal (self-citation) it can increase the impact factor. Notwithstanding, it is assumed that a high-impact factor reflects the high standard and quality of a journal.

Furthermore, imagine you submit a thesis on job satisfaction and your most recently cited article is 2007. What this means is that your research is likely going to be a replication because you may not have conducted a thorough literature search. As much as possible, make sure you are up to date in the subject area, and cite recent (and relevant) publications in your work. Some examiners will return work to you if they do not consider it current enough. I recommend that you do a quick internet search to check recent developments in your research area, even if these were published too late to go in your thesis. It can help if you know a bit about the new research before meeting an examiner (Shaw, 2017).

In support of these ten tips on examiners' expectations, Golding et al. (2014, p.566) explain that viva examiners tend to:

1 be generally consistent
2 expect a thesis to meet the requirements for the PhD award
3 decide whether a thesis will pass or not after reviewing the first few chapters
4 read a thesis objectively, both as an academic and as a layperson
5 be infuriated and upset by grammatical and punctuation errors
6 favour an articulate research work
7 favour a study that draws on the relevant literature
8 favour a study that justifies the methodology
9 favour a study that connects with the findings
10 require a thesis to merit publication
11 give objective feedback and guidance on further improvement.

Facing difficult examiners

Just as in businesses where we hear about demanding customers and horrible bosses, during your viva examination you may meet examiners who can be difficult. It is therefore essential to know how to handle them. As you will just be meeting them for the first time and do not know much about them, the critical point you need to focus on is your 'attitude'.

Well, allow me to share my experience with a difficult examiner. In the first year of registration on a PhD programme, all candidates are normally on probation. At the end of the first year we undertake a transfer interview (oral defence) where examiners assess the draft chapters of our theses.

The outcome of the transfer interview is normally one of the four options:

1 recommendation for termination of studies
2 transfer to MPhil
3 be given a further six months to prepare a revised thesis
4 continue on the PhD programme (University of Leicester, 2011)

Back to the story. We had an examiner who appeared to be tough with students during the upgrade/transfer interview. She would say things like 'This work is absolute rubbish.' Her comments made some students cry, while others became aggressive towards her. Each time students came out of her oral examination they would be upset and angry. She also took issue with a student who had dressed very casually for the interview. For most of their conversation they argued about his clothing. So, by the time they got round to the real business of defending his draft chapters, this would have thrown him and affected the coherency of his thoughts/arguments.

Each time a student came out of an interview with this lady I would approach them and ask, 'How did it go?' I was gathering all the questions they were asked because I was preparing for the day I would also get to meet her for my defence. At last, the day arrived. It was my turn to meet with her and another examiner. My supervisor was also present. Supervisors are not allowed to comment during the examination process unless they have been specifically asked to do so. They are present just to make a note of the comments so that they can discuss these later with their students and implement changes where necessary.

On that day, I was dressed in a suit and tie. Then, when I entered the meeting room, I greeted them, and they welcomed me. After the usual questions and responses (please refer to Chapter 12 for the list of possible questions for mock viva/final viva) they asked me to step outside so they could deliberate, and said they would call me back in for the final verdict. While I was going out she said to me, 'While you are waiting, think about what you think our decision will be, and when we invite you back you can tell us.'

I went out and sat in the waiting room. After 15 minutes I was invited back in. The first question she asked me was, 'So what do you think our verdict is?' I told them that 'Because I responded correctly to most of your questions, I would expect to be given a pass mark.' I then added, 'However, if you asked me to go back and start this work afresh, I would be more than happy to do so. This is because I know you are here to help me get my thesis to the expected standard required. For this reason, I would start afresh if it is the opinion of experts like yourselves that I should do so.' Nodding her head in astonishment she said, 'I like that attitude.' She continued, 'Well, I have good news for you. You do not have to do any corrections. Carry on with your work and all the best in your studies.' This reminds me of the Bobby Unser quote that 'Success is where preparation and opportunity meet' (cited in Shannon, 2017).

All along I was preparing by:

1 asking people who had gone in before me
2 learning from and avoiding the mistakes made by others
3 learning from the success stories of those who had gone in before me.

This prepared me to face – and overcome – the 'dreaded' examiner.

So some examiners not only test your academic prowess but your attitude as well. They want to see how you respond to criticism. They do so because they know there are other examiners out there to test you on these grounds. This was good preparation for me because this experience paid off during my final viva voce. My external examiner was also very tough, but I remained calm, and where I did not agree with him I backed it up (politely) with evidence. At the end of the viva it was all joy and laughter as we had a group photograph.

Dos and don'ts of a successful viva

Dos

1 Do undertake personal revision and practise how to respond to the list of viva questions.
2 Do get friends and colleagues to look at your work and provide feedback.
3 Do conduct a mock viva with colleagues and friends who have passed through a similar viva experience. This helps to create a real-life experience and you can ask for feedback on what is expected of certain questions.
4 Do search for information about your examiners. Review their publications and use information that is relevant to your thesis. If you know your examiners early enough before your final submission, I recommend citing their papers, if it directly relates to your research, or if it supports an argument/statement in your thesis. Ensure that you properly cite them and avoid misrepresenting them. Citations are important for academics, especially when we consider the journal's visibility, quality of the paper and author's influence in the area (Szomszor et al., 2020). Researching your examiners will help you to:
   • review papers they have published
   • cite their work if it relates to your work and you find the content useful

- understand how they structure their arguments in a paper
- understand their research strengths
- find mutual friends – for example, in searching for information about my external examiner I noticed we had a friend in common (a PhD student at another university). I asked my friend about the examiner and he said the same person was his supervisor (it's a small world). He then told me that his strengths were literature review and methodology. I found this very helpful.

5   Do a quick internet check for recent developments in your research area, even if these were published too late to go in your thesis, it can help if you know a bit about them at the viva (Shaw, 2017).

6   Do bookmark your thesis chapters with Post-it notes. Make a note of the key points in each chapter on the Post-it notes. You should also write the page numbers where the information can be found in your thesis.

7   Do check out the venue for the viva before the day. This will give you an idea of the seating arrangement and atmosphere.

8   Do have enough rest the day before the viva. Make sure you get at least six hours of sleep.

9   Do make sure you prepare a one-page summary (preferably short bullet points) of answers to key viva questions which you should have in front of you during the viva – for example, a list of key authors that influenced your research, main theoretical arguments, major findings, theoretical and practical contributions, justification for sampling, statistical analysis, validity and reliability, limitations and how you attempted to address them. Sometimes you may know the answers, but because you are nervous you tend to forget. In situations like these, the one-page summary might be all you need to get back on track.

10   Do dress smartly (formal/semi-formal). As the saying goes, 'Dress the way you want to be addressed.'

11   Do gather all the resources you will need for the viva – e.g. a pen, jotter, a printed copy of your thesis which should be the same version submitted to the examiners. If you have updated your thesis after submission, please bring the exact copy you submitted and not the updated copy. Of course, you can also print the updated version to bring along just in case you want to let them know about the changes you have made, including any errors you may have already corrected.

12   Do arrive at the venue at least 45 minutes before the start time.

13   Do remember to switch your mobile phone off.

14   Do remember that the general principle of your choice of data for analysis is that every figure or statistic you choose should have a reason behind it and is open for debate/question by an external examiner. You should be prepared to defend your choices, even those which may seem trivial – such as the percentage of non-responses to your questionnaire (Koenigsberger, 2015).

15 Do remember that you are in charge – it's your research, and you have to justify it. Be ready to explain any aspect – your choice of research area, selection of interview subjects, research material, methodology, results you obtained, and so on. Of course, you know much more about this than the examiners. A common flaw with candidates is that they assume the examiners know more than they actually do, so the candidate fails to justify what they found because they don't see that they have to explain it (Shaw, 2017).

16 Do remember that the examiners are aware that you may be nervous, but work on controlling your nerves.

17 Do think carefully about the question before responding. If you are not clear about the question, politely ask the examiner to rephrase or repeat it.

18 Do speak clearly, audibly and moderately enough to convey your message.

19 Do maintain eye contact with the examiners. Eye contact increases connection with your audience giving you huge control of the environment. How do you achieve this? When speaking, don't just alternate between one person and another in a haphazard manner. Do it systematically. For example, when explaining a thought you can focus on one examiner at the point when you pause your speaking, then you can focus on the next examiner and then carry on speaking.

20 Do keep your initial answers simple. How would you explain what you have been researching the past few years to a layperson?

21 Do remember that no one knows your chosen research area as well as you do, which is both an advantage and a disadvantage. It's an advantage because you have the stage to explain something you have spent much time exploring. It's a disadvantage in that the external assessors won't be that familiar with some aspects of your work – so anything that might be less familiar to an outsider has to be clearly set out and explained, even if you think it's obvious (Shaw, 2017).

22 Do refer examiners to evidence/arguments in your thesis that support the question you have been asked. Allow your thesis to speak for you. Remember that examiners sometimes want to be sure you are the author of your thesis. So, in addition to responding to their questions, you can refer them to specific information on specific pages. This tells them how familiar you are with your work. For example, you could say, 'I refer you to page 65, where I justified the use of the Mann–Whitney U Test as opposed to the T-test'.

23 Do know that it is okay if you cannot remember a specific answer to a question. It's fine to say you will come back to that question shortly as you are trying to put your thoughts together.

24 Do ask for time out to refresh yourself (if needed). Observe the tempo and know when to request time out. It could be immediately after you have responded to a question that was asked. And since you still have the floor to speak, you can then politely make the request. For example, I did make

a request to use the toilet because I had finished four bottles of water that were placed in front of me. The examiners even joked about it, asking if I needed more water.

25 Do anticipate negative feedback – but view it as constructive criticism.

26 Do expect to meet difficult examiners.

27 Do prepare to ask questions. Some examiners might give you the opportunity to ask questions. For example, after the gruelling interview session I was asked by the internal examiner, 'Do you have any questions? Or is there anything you think we should have addressed?'

Don'ts

1 Don't take a different version of your thesis to the one submitted to the examiners. I made this error during my mock viva. After my thesis was submitted to the examiners, I went through my work, found some errors and edited it. I brought the updated version to the exam. So, whenever I referred the examiners to a page, because I had updated my version the page numbers were different from the version my examiners had. This made me appear very clumsy. For example, I would say, 'I refer you to page 25, where I explained . . .', whereas on the examiner's version it would be 'page 23', and she would not be able to find the information I was referring to. This was embarrassing. Thankfully, it was just a mock viva. I did not repeat the same mistake in my final viva.

2 Don't be confrontational. Rather, present your case in a convincing and polite manner. Where you tend to disagree, make sure you have evidence to back up your viewpoint.

3 Don't be afraid to ask the examiners to repeat or rephrase questions if you do not understand.

4 Don't memorize answers because nervousness can make you have a brain-freeze. A student explained how she was knocked off her feet in a viva exam having memorized all her answers. When she stepped in, she thought that the first question she was going to be asked was, 'Tell us about your research'. Instead, she was confronted for using a poor research design, and because she did not expect this in the opening question, it threw her off balance.

5 Don't always consult your thesis to respond to questions. There should be a balance. Imagine if for every question you are asked, you start flipping the pages of your thesis to find answers before responding. This will give the impression that you may not be genuinely involved in the research. Do it sparingly – your thesis should speak for you to demonstrate you have a grasp of its contents.

6 Don't put on clothing that will make you feel uncomfortable. For example, putting on tight shoes can spoil your interview because your attention will be diverted to the inconvenience.

7 Don't chew gum or talk with a sweet in your mouth during the viva. Many a time people want to feel fresh by taking something minty. This should be thrown away before you go into the exam.

8 Don't forget to thank the examiners, regardless of the outcome. Appreciate them for their constructive feedback and express your desire to work on the corrections as soon as possible.

Online viva and meetings

I have itemized the dos and don'ts in the preceding section to ensure you succeed at your physical viva. However, there may be instances where you or the examiners are unable to attend a physical meeting. For example, many people have now started working from their homes due to concern about coronavirus. So, just as you would prepare for a face-to-face viva or meeting with your supervisor, planning for online meetings is equally important.

Whatever the reasons for scheduling online meetings, I would recommend you do the following:

1 **Familiarize yourself with the meeting application.** You should familiarize yourself with the online tool to be used for the meeting (e.g. Skype, Google Meet, Zoom, WebEx, GoToMeeting, Microsoft Teams). It can be frustrating, and sometimes could be seen as a lack of seriousness on your part, if you begin to learn how to use the online platform during the meeting.

2 **Have a good internet connection.** You should ensure you have a very good internet connection and enough mobile data, if you are using your phone's internet. During the 'stay at home' government's advice as a result of the coronavirus pandemic, I was teaching from home and observed that some students had problems joining the class due to network fluctuations and poor internet connections.

3 **Prioritize your overall personal appearance and maintain a quiet environment.** Most times, as you will be sitting in the comfort of your home, there is a tendency for you to want to dress too informally. Please take this meeting as seriously as the face-to-face meeting that you would have had to physically attend. Furthermore, as you will be at home, there is a possibility that your children or pet may occasionally pop in and distract you. Please keep these interruptions to the barest minimum. Also, your surrounding environment should look presentable with good lighting. For me personally, I sit with my back to the wall and I always make sure the room is bright enough (without any shadows on my face).

4 **Ensure your PC complies with the app.** Not all computers will automatically comply with some apps. For example, in one of my recent online classes I used a MacBook and could not enable my camera for my students to see me. I had to change to another PC to address this problem. So, always carry out a test to ensure all the features (for example audio, mic, video) are working well.

Chapter 11: summary

In this chapter, the author provided a guide to help you and your supervisor select an external examiner. He also recommended ways in which you could make it easier for the examiner to read your work. The author also offered useful strategies for dealing with difficult examiners and succeeding in your viva.

It is assumed that you are now set for your viva, and in the next and final chapter, I share sample viva questions to help you practise with your peers and senior academics. The learning point here is to give you real-life experience of the whole viva process.

12 The viva experience

By the end of this chapter, you will be able to:

1 Approach the viva as an examination
2 Understand how examiners critique your work
3 Use the sample questions to practise with other students, staff and friends
4 Explain how you have met the key criterion of 'originality'

My viva experience – typical of what happens

In the previous chapter I highlighted a number of dos and don'ts to achieving a successful viva outcome. In this chapter I would like to share my own experience of the viva, to give you an insight into the way my interview (oral exam) progressed. However, before I proceed, I would like to remind you of the possible results from a viva voce examination:

1 You pass without any correction – this, I must point out, rarely happens.
2 You pass with minor corrections – you will be given about three months within which to revise and resubmit your work.
3 You pass with major corrections – a second viva may be scheduled, for which you will be granted about 12 months to make the necessary changes to your work and resubmit it.
4 You fail, but the examiners recommend you for an MPhil award.
5 You fail, but the examiners recommend you for an MPhil award, subject to minor corrections – you will be given about three months to make the changes and resubmit your work.
6 You fail – the work does not merit even an MPhil.

Now that we have seen the possible outcomes, let me share my experience. You see, when you are in the 'hot seat' you might not realize how much time has passed. The interview format is an engaging event which, to some candidates, can seem to take forever. So, before my own interview was due to commence, I noted down the start time, and after the session I checked how long the interview had lasted. The entire session lasted two hours, followed by a 50-minute intermission for the panellists to make their outcome recommendations.

On entering the interview room I was greeted by the chair, the internal examiner, the external examiner and my supervisor. Before I continue, allow me to introduce you to each interview panellist, their position and role.

The chair is usually a senior member of the academic staff at your university. Their role is to moderate the exercise and ensure that the university's guidelines are followed. They are not, however, expected to interview you. The internal examiner is an academic member of your university appointed by the PhD programme leader. They are expected to be active in research, with relevant expertise in the student's field of study. Depending on the university, the internal examiner may be responsible for scheduling a date for the viva in consultation with the external examiner and the student. Although the external examiner is an academic staff member from another university, they have pertinent expertise in the student's research area and are expected to have extensive research experience in examining PhD students. In essence, the examiners write their independent reports on a submitted thesis. Then, after the viva voce, they write a joint report of the outcome and their recommendations.

If you are a university staff member and doing your PhD at the same institution, the university will be required to appoint two external examiners (instead of the usual internal and external examiner). This practice is implemented so as to ensure the examination process is fair and not influenced by any preferential treatment assumptions in the process of your interview.

The supervisor, as you may already know, is the academic staff member with all the necessary expertise in your research area who has mentored you from the start of your academic journey through to your viva and subsequent graduation. It is not compulsory for your supervisor to attend the viva as they neither take on an active role nor speak during the interview. The supervisor merely observes the process. If you want your supervisor to be present during the viva, you may need to notify the PhD programme leader. In my case, I wanted my supervisor present during the course of the interview because his presence was going to boost my morale. Furthermore, it is generally good for your supervisor to observe the process because they will have an opportunity to make useful notes, which can be referred to as discussion points in subsequent corrections.

Let me now resume the insight into the interview process. After the greeting and exchange of pleasantries, the following conversation ensued.

I was asked if I understood the purpose of the oral exam and what to expect, to which I replied 'yes'. I then initiated the interview by acknowledging that the meeting was to present the thesis as the result of my own work; that I would clarify any concerns raised or ambiguities identified by the examiners in relation to my thesis; that I was ready to show the expertise through which I had systematically carried out my research; that I possessed a thorough understanding of the models, theories and research methods I had used; and, finally, that I had acquired and interpreted new knowledge through original research, in a manner which would demonstrate my confidence and the ability to inform and convince the examiners. Now, you may think that this list of interview points involved an extensive period of talk time; in reality, it took all but three minutes to deliver.

Next, I was asked by the exam panel to tell them about my research. The question you are likely to hear at this stage is either 'What is your research about?' or 'Can you summarize your thesis for us?' Preparation for this is imperative. Before the viva I had already practised my response to both question options repeatedly, always timing myself on a stopwatch so that I would not go over four minutes in my answer.

You should aim to keep your answers brief and straight to the point, making sure you touch on the following:

- Firstly, I talked about my motivation. I explained what inspired me to do this piece of research, presented the reason for choosing the topic and why I thought it was important.
- Secondly, I gave a brief overview of my background along with the requisite knowledge and skills that guided me in undertaking the study.
- Finally, I explained how I intended to answer my main research question. This included talking about what I did to collect my data, how I analysed the information and which research tools I used in the process; what I concluded; the implications of my findings; and, lastly, what made my work original in terms of new knowledge and contribution to knowledge.

Remember, you must keep it brief. Be aware that while there are standardized sample questions to guide you, examiners might approach or ask questions specific to your research. Furthermore, bear in mind that they will have already spent about a month or two reading your thesis thoroughly. That is the very time during which they will have collated questions requiring clarification. Also note that if you are given the opportunity to summarize your thesis, they might continue on from where you stopped talking and then probe further into what you had just said.

You may not always be asked to summarize your thesis. You may also not be asked questions that you have familiarized yourself with, and for that reason it is best not to try to memorize your answers. Otherwise, in the heat of the moment, sometimes one can experience brain-freeze, or even be unable to recollect what one had planned to say. A colleague once shared with me a bad experience during her viva. She was under the impression that they would start with the usual question of 'Tell us about your thesis', which she had prepared to deliver in the opening minutes. Instead, the external examiner opened with a strong statement of 'How can you make such a statement?', pointing to a section in her thesis. Finding herself unprepared for this kind of opening question, it threw her off balance straightaway and she began to stutter. As mentioned before, preparation is key, but memorizing your answers is not.

Back to my experience. I was asked to explain why I used the theories that influenced my research. In preparation for the interview, while reviewing sample viva questions, I anticipated the possibility of being asked 'Which authors influenced your study?', and so I prepared for it by making a summary table of the key authors who were vital to my work. In my case, the external examiner expressed concerns about the theories, stating that more updated models had been developed, which he believed I could have used instead. So I had to justify the models I had applied in my research, citing their strengths and significance to my study. I also clarified that, in trying to address my research problem, it was easier to compare 'like for like' – i.e. compare my findings to the findings of previous research on the same subject matter.

I was also asked to explain why I used the Mann–Whitney U Test for my data analysis. In response, I listed and explained a number of relevant statistical tools that could have been used, and why I had employed the Mann–Whitney U Test as the preferred analytical instrument. The reasons included the nature of my data and how suitable and easy it was to use the tool.

After an exhaustive but satisfactorily response, the chair asked if the examiners had further questions. The internal examiner then turned to me and asked if there were any questions I thought they should have asked, but did not. That, as I saw it, was a good opportunity to let them know about the extra work invested in my thesis review. So I told the panel that, in my submitted thesis, I had stated that I had used a *positivist* philosophy in my research, when, in fact, I should have stated that I had used a *pragmatist* philosophy. I brought this to their attention, informing them that I wrote this at the early stage of my research because I had planned to use only quantitative methods. But, with hindsight, I adopted mixed methods because they would provide more depth and better understanding of the research problem. I pointed out that I had made the necessary corrections which, with their permission, I wished to include when resubmitting the amended thesis.

As you may have noted, it is good practice to go over your research thoroughly, even after you have submitted it. However, when you identify errors and make corrections I would advise you to take a hard copy of the already submitted version to the viva. It will be easier to refer to relevant sections or pages when prompted – a recently corrected version might result in changes to page numbers, and this could lead to confusion. For example, while looking at the submitted thesis evidence, the examiner might say 'On page 50, you stated . . .', whereas in your amended version the section being referred to could now be on page 52. An inconsistency such as this will inevitably make it difficult for you and the examiner to reconcile the pages.

The panellists also asked if I was aware of any recently published research available after I had submitted my thesis. Again, while anticipating this question in my interview preparation, I had performed a brief yet sufficient web search and used thesis key words to search journal databases. I was able to find a publication which I could refer to, thus confidently explaining how different my findings were in relation to it while also citing the strengths of my research. I informed the examiners that I had already referred to the new publication in the literature review of my updated thesis.

In the end, after a gruelling two-hour exercise, I was asked to take a break while the examiners deliberated the outcome. After about 50 minutes, I was invited back in and told the words I was longing to hear: 'Congratulations! You have passed. However, there are a few corrections you must make and resubmit within eight weeks.'

In summary, I was asked to make the following corrections:

1 To make clearer the links in the literature review between the seminal contributions, ensuring that they were followed through in the conceptual framework, methods used and data acquired.
2 To more clearly articulate the strengths and weaknesses of the Herzberg and Hackman & Oldham models of motivation, and the rationale for integrating these two models.
3 To elaborate more fully on the link(s) between the nature of the data and the decision to use the Mann–Whitney U Test in the data analysis.
4 To revisit the discussion, conclusions and recommendations, and to consider and reflect on how the three-factor (combined) model may be amended in the light of current research findings.
5 To ensure the specific contributions to knowledge were more clearly articulated in the study's conclusions and recommendations.
6 As a candidate, to feel encouraged to include such minor improvements as deemed appropriate to enhancing the quality of the thesis.

All in all, my viva was a memorable experience, so much so that I felt encouraged to ask for a photo opportunity with the panellists. They obliged. I beamed with an unforgettable feeling of pride and success.

Well, I shall leave you with some viva 'survival' tips based on my experience.

Whenever I was asked a question which I could not immediately respond to, I would take a few sips of water to give myself time to think in those few, precious split seconds. By the time I put the cup down, I had put my thoughts together, ready to begin my response. This 'buying time' technique needs to be planned systematically, however. While there were occasions when I bought time by sipping water, there were other times (twice, in fact) when asking the examiners to repeat the question worked just as well.

Be careful how much water you drink though. My clever technique got to a stage where I had finished all the bottles of water on the table. Must I really spell out what happened next!? As the next question was asked, I appealed to the exam board for a short break – to answer the call of nature. It was both a funny and an awkward moment as they all laughed at the same time, surprised that I, the examinee, was bold enough to stop them, the examiners, midway to request a break. When I returned, they asked jokingly if I wanted more water.

Here is a take-home tip about maintaining eye contact while speaking at a clearly elocuted pace. For example, whenever an examiner asked me a question I would maintain eye contact with that person while answering. As soon as I had finished speaking on a specific point, I would pause, shift my glance to another examiner, establish eye contact, and continue speaking further. If you are responding to only one examiner at a time, the others may feel somewhat alienated, wanting attention. Pause for thought here – if you are talking and repeatedly turning back and forth from one examiner to the other, you might unintentionally resemble an oscillating desktop fan, which will make you look far less composed and far more anxious. The one-to-one eye contact technique I have shared is also helpful in noticing whether the listener is paying attention to what you have to say or not. For instance, while explaining a point to the external examiner, I noticed that the person was reading a section in my thesis. Rather than feeling intimidated, I decided to face the other panellists whom I could look in the eye while speaking.

Sample viva questions

In the previous section, I gave an account of my viva experience. It is important to note that there are no hard and fast rules on how the viva is conducted. Each student's experience will probably be different. The Doctor of Philosophy degree by Research is awarded by an academic institution to students who demonstrate competence by justifying the following:

1 Research context
2 Research methods
3 Data analysis, findings and discussions
4 Originality and research implications

Therefore, the practice questions presented in this section are based on the author's personal experience and ideas from other academic resources (e.g. University of Leicester, n.d. a; Clough and Ferguson, 2009; Berry, 2012; Guccione and Wellington, 2017) to help you prepare for your viva.

General questions

1 Tell us about your research/summarize your thesis.
2 Why did you choose this topic?
3 What motivated you to write your thesis? In other words, who or what was the main reason for your investigation?
4 What do you find interesting about your research?/Name three interesting points from your investigation.
5 What new knowledge did you learn by conducting this study?
6 Were there any surprises as you progressed?
7 How has doing this research changed your views as a researcher?
8 What new knowledge has your work brought to light?
9 What are the strengths of your research?

10 What are the limitations of your study?
11 Why do you believe your thesis should be published in an academic journal?
12 Explain how your study has advanced knowledge in theory, policy or practice.
13 What aspect of your research would you change if you had to undertake the study again?
14 Why do you deserve the PhD award?

Research context

1 What are the major debates underpinning your research?
2 Name five of the most influential theorists who contributed to your investigation.
3 What criteria influenced your selection of the sources used? In other words, how did you ensure the quality of the literature sources?
4 What is your contribution to knowledge?
5 Do you have evidence of 'Theory ABC' linked in your discussion?
6 Is there any recent development in this field since you submitted your thesis that could be included?
7 What is unique about your research framework?
8 Can you explain the relevance of 'Theory ABC' in this study?
9 What factors influenced your choice of research questions?
10 What factors led to your hypotheses?
11 Are you aware of any further studies on your topic since the publication of your research?

Research methods

1 What criteria influenced your selection of the research method(s) used?
2 What data did you collect for each of your research objectives?
3 Did you use the same data-collection methods for all your research objectives?
4 How did you select your sample size? In other words, give the rationale for your sample size.
5 Is your sample size large enough for the analysis?
6 How did you collect the data?
7 What were the challenges of data collection?
8 Were there any surprises in your data? Did your data turnout as you expected?
9 Why was your research method necessary?
10 What ethical issues did you take into consideration in conducting the research?
11 How did you choose your analytical tool?

Analysis and findings

1 Explain how you analysed your data.
2 What challenges did you experience during your data analysis?
3 Provide three examples of how your data is linked to your research questions.
4 Summarize your findings.
5 How did you ensure that your research method and data are reliable and valid?

Discussion

1 How do your findings compare with previous studies?
2 How does your investigation tie in with your literature review?
3 What is unique about your study?
4 Can you generalize your findings?
5 Have you published aspects of your research en route to completing your PhD?

Conclusions/Implications

1 What are the implications of your findings to theory and practice?
2 How would your study influence fellow academics and practitioners?
3 What are the limitations of your study and what measures did you take to address these shortcomings?
4 What recommendations would you make to extend or develop this study?
5 Are there any other questions that you expected us to ask you?

Chapter 12: summary

This concluding chapter provided sample questions to help you prepare for your viva examination. The author shared his experience to help you understand how examiners might critique your work. It is vital to use the sample questions to practise with other students, staff and friends. More importantly, remember that the key criterion of 'originality' is what your PhD must demonstrate. Good luck!

Appendices

Before my final viva, I used some sample viva questions to summarize my thesis onto two sheets of A4-size paper which I took with me to the viva voce examination. Table 1 summarizes my research, while Tables 2, 3 and 4 comprise the authors that influenced my study – with emphasis on the research topic, the methods, the findings, and how these articles compared with mine. You will note that I included the page numbers where these articles have been cited in my thesis; it helped me to navigate my research quickly and with ease when referring the examiners to specific sections. To ease understanding, the tables presented in this section run over a few pages. However, in practice, you can create an abridged template that fits on just two sheets of A4-size paper. That way, you will have fewer papers – apart from your thesis – to flip through during your mock and final viva examinations.

Appendix A

A guide to summarizing your thesis

Table 1 My research summary for the viva voce examination

What is my research about?	Turnover has continued to cause disruption in organizations, for instance:
	The costs associated with the recruitment and training of new employees.
	The loss in productivity as a result of the void created by the employees that leave.
	The primary reason for turnover has been attributed to job dissatisfaction.
	Several studies have shown that the universities in Nigeria are not exempt from this problem.
	There is a high turnover at Nigerian universities, mostly due to dissatisfaction with intrinsic and extrinsic factors.
What did I do?	As a management consultant by profession, I help organizations to get the best from their employees through research, training and benchmarking good practices.
	Education is the bedrock of national development.
	Lecturers are at the forefront of the field of research, preparing individuals for employment and formal dissemination of knowledge.
	Therefore, I was very much interested in looking for alternative approaches to addressing lecturers' job dissatisfaction and its consequences, which leads to staff turnover.
	I surveyed lecturers at public and private universities in the North Central Region. I also conducted interviews to get more understanding to support the survey data.
	I analysed the interview data using thematic analysis to get patterns from the responses.
	I also tested the four hypotheses using the Mann–Whitney U Test to check for any significant differences in intrinsic and extrinsic job dimensions and turnover intentions between public and private universities.

(continued)

Table 1 Continued

What did I find?	While there were no significant variations in intrinsic, extrinsic and core job dimensions, there was a statistically significant difference in turnover intention.
	More private university lecturers wanted to leave their jobs than public university lecturers because of higher job security at public universities, and access to the tertiary education fund that was not available at private universities.
	Another factor was the absence of trade unions at private universities, but not at public universities.
	Other significant findings:
	Private university lecturers had more opportunities to practise their skills than public university lecturers.
	There were better working conditions at private universities than public universities.
	Also, the topmost reasons why public and private university lecturers might want to leave their jobs were similar:
	inadequate fringe benefits
	personal reasons
	dissatisfaction with salary
	insufficient funding for research.
	The four main reasons for dissatisfaction at both public and private universities were:
	work overload
	inadequate funding for research and scholarship
	small office space
	inadequate work facilities.
Why does that matter?	In line with these findings, I have made recommendations to university management, the government and other stakeholders on how to address the dissatisfaction at Nigerian universities.
	I proposed practical strategies to apply my model.
	I also advised benchmarking some of the good practices that led to high job satisfaction (e.g. recognition for performance at private university).
Why is my research unique?	Primary data/developed research instrument.
	Conceptual framework – my research establishes a three-factor model.
	Findings: I have identified other variables that affect job satisfaction not previously considered, such as the findings from task significance and skill variety.

Appendix B

Summarizing literature sources

Table 2 Key authors that influenced my study on Nigerian universities (country-specific literature sources)

Author/ Journal	Research focus	Method(s) used	Findings
Fapohunda (2012) This author is cited in my thesis on the following pages: 2, 74, 75, 67, 159, 164, 167, 180, 190.	Compared pay disparity and pay satisfaction	Survey Sampled 200 academic staff Five hypotheses tests Using chi-square Four universities in south-west Nigeria (two public and two private) Quantitative	The significant difference in pay disparity and pay satisfaction was noted in private universities pay being better than public universities pay. Private respondents were somewhat more satisfied with their pay than public universities. Working conditions between public and private universities differed. However, the explanation did not show the direction of the difference (e.g. private better than public). Private universities have more training and development opportunities within and outside. (Contrary to my findings, public universities had more opportunities because of the Nigerian government's Tertiary Education Trust Fund – TET-Fund.) Private university academics are more motivated than public university lecturers – thus supporting aspects (e.g. recognition) in my research.

(continued)

Table 2 Continued

Gbenu (2013) This author is cited in my thesis on the following pages: 2, 3, 76, 159, 171, 190, 194.	Academic staff turnover and national development	Analysis of secondary sources	Suggests that scarce resources, underfunding, brain drain and staff turnover are the most crucial and central to the crises in the Nigerian university system. Explains that policy rigidity, unsatisfactory working environment, delayed promotion, disappointing salaries, inadequate welfare packages, poor research activities, and rigid leadership behaviour lead to the low retention rate of workers and low productivity. (Provided base for my research objectives) mine is a comparative study – benchmarking good practices.
Ologunde et al. (2013) The authors are cited in my thesis on the following pages: 4, 9, 168.	Moonlighting among university lecturers	Survey – questionnaire Sample 347 lecturers from six universities (four public and two private) in south-west Correlation, T-test and ANOVA used Quantitative	There is a significant difference between the performance of the university teachers who moonlight and those who do not, in south-western universities. The performance of those who moonlight is negatively affected. (Provided base for my research based on the current situation at public universities.)

Table 2 Continued

Ologunde et al. (2007) The authors are cited in my thesis on the following pages: 2, 3, 5, 9, 190.	Labour turnover at universities in south-west Nigeria	Sample 442 lecturers from four universities (two federal and two state) Survey T-test and two-way ANOVA The analysis is based on intrinsic and extrinsic variables Quantitative	Poor motivation affected labour turnover of university teachers. Also, the motivation strategies available for university teachers in Nigeria are inadequate for their continued stay in the university system. My research is more in-depth with interviews to get more explanation. My research establishes a three-factor model. I have identified other variables that affect job satisfaction not previously considered, such as the findings from task signifi-cance and skill variety.
Satope and Akintunde (2013) The authors are cited in my thesis on the following pages: 5, 67, 190.	Factors of labour mobility in Nigerian universities	The survey in south-west Nigeria 98 academics Quantitative	Attracting and retaining academics is a challenge. The primary reason for mobility is the new pension scheme and university expansion system.
Iornem (2014) This author is cited in my thesis on page 9.	Motivation and job satisfaction of secondary school teachers in Kaduna	Qualitative research Pearson product-moment correlation coefficient Chi-square Weighted averages	Significant differences in motivation and job satisfac-tion of teachers at public and private schools. Significant differences in job satisfaction of male and female teachers.

Table 3 Other key authors that influenced my study

Author	Research focus	Method(s) used	Findings
Oshagbemi and Hickson (2003) These authors are cited in my thesis on the following pages: 17, 37.	Overall job satisfaction of academics in UK universities	Survey Binomial logistics 554 usable questionnaires	There was a positive relationship between pay satisfaction and gender. Women were more satisfied than men. Research and pay satisfaction positively associated with rank.
Oshagbemi (1999)	Academics and their managers: a comparative study	Sampled 566 intrinsic and extrinsic analysis	There was no difference in administration and management, research, and present pay. The was a significant difference in teaching, co-workers' behaviour, head of units' behaviour, physical conditions/working facilities, and promotions.
Ssesanga and Garrett (2005) The authors are cited in my thesis on the following pages: 17, 37, 40, 172, 186, 191.	Job satisfaction of academics: perspectives from Uganda	Sampled 182 from two universities Intrinsic and extrinsic analysis	Finds that any factor, be it intrinsic or extrinsic, can affect satisfaction. Contradicts Herzberg. (My research also contradicts Herzberg; the difference is the three-factor model and my methods.)

Table 3 Continued

Herzberg et al. (1959) Herzberg (1987) The authors are cited in my thesis on the following pages: 37, 38, 164, 172, 190, 192.	Motivation and job satisfaction		The theory states that job satisfaction and dissatisfaction are affected by two different sets of factors.
Hackman and Oldham (1976, 1980) The authors are cited in my thesis on the following pages: 41, 42, 72, 73, 174, 176, 192.	Motivation through work or job redesign	Job diagnostic survey (using motivating potential score) Means, standard deviation and correlation	How jobs can be redesigned to improve productivity. High 5 core job dimensions can lead to high job satisfaction and low turnover.
Mobley (1977) This author is cited in my thesis on the following pages: 47, 48, 100.	Relationship between job satisfaction and employee turnover		Mobley (1977) holds the view that when employees are unhappy with their jobs, they begin to search for alternative employment. Mobley's model (1977) provides a decision process that employees follow in deciding whether to stay in a job or quit.

Table 4 New research development after thesis submission (before the viva)

Author	Research focus	Method(s) used	Findings
Bello et al. (2017) The authors are cited in my thesis on the following pages: 14 and 72.	A comparative study of academic staff job satisfaction in public and private universities in Nigeria	Surveyed 120 lecturers T-test Two universities (one public and one private) Landmark University and University of Ilorin	Private universities have better working conditions. Public universities have better payment packages. Private university lecturers are recognized more. Recommendations to the Nigerian government to intervene and make incentive benefits available to private universities.
Umaru and Ombugus (2017) The authors are cited in my thesis on page 14.	Job satisfaction of lecturers	Surveyed 167 lecturers Quantitative T-test	Regular salary payment, promotion opportunities, work environment, attainment of work goals, the opportunity for growth and development, among others, are the determinants of job satisfaction of college of education lecturers.

References

American Psychological Association (2010). *Publication Manual of the American Psychological Association*, 6th edn. Washington, DC: American Psychological Association.

Anglia Ruskin University (2019). *University Library: Guide to Harvard style of Referencing* [pdf]. Available at: https://libweb.anglia.ac.uk/referencing/files/Harvard_referencing_201718.pdf (Accessed: 25 May 2020).

Apsimon, O. (2013). Comment on: White, J.S. What is the average length of a doctoral thesis? *Research Gate*. [Online]. Comment posted 2013. Available at: https://www.researchgate.net/post/What_is_the_average_length_of_a_doctoral_thesis (Accessed: 11 June 2020).

Bazrafkan, L., Shokrpour, N., Yousefi, A. and Yamani, N. (2016). Management of stress and anxiety among PhD students during thesis writing: a qualitative study. *The Health Care Manager*, 35(3), pp.231–40.

Bello, A.O., Ogundipe, O.M. and Eze, S.C. (2017). Employee job satisfaction in Nigerian tertiary institution: a comparative study of academic staff in public and private universities. *Global Journal of Human Resource Management*, 5(4), pp.33–46.

Berry, D. (2012). The Graduate School guide to … surviving the viva [pdf], *University of Reading*. Available at: https://www.reading.ac.uk/web/files/graduateschool/GSG_SurvivingTheViva.pdf (Accessed: 25 May 2020).

Brownlow, S. (1997). Going the extra mile: the rewards of publishing your undergraduate research. *Psi Chi Journal of Undergraduate Research*, 2(3), pp.83–5.

Cardiff Metropolitan University (2018). Research degree regulations [PhD and MPhil], in *Academic Handbook 2017/18*, Vol. 1. Available at: https://www.cardiffmet.ac.uk/registry/academichandbook/Documents/AH1_11_01.pdf (Accessed: 25 May 2020).

Cardiff Metropolitan University (2019). Code of practice on plagiarism, in *Academic Handbook 2019/20*, Vol. 1. Available at: https://www.cardiffmet.ac.uk/registry/academichandbook/Documents/AH1_08_05.pdf (Accessed: 21 May 2020).

Clough, G. and Ferguson, R. (2009). Top 40 potential viva questions. *Research Essentials* [Online]. Available at: http://www.open.ac.uk/blogs/ResearchEssentials/?p=156 (Accessed: 25 May 2020).

Covey, S.R. (2004). *The 7 Habits of Highly Effective People: Restoring the Character Ethic*. New York: Free Press.

Cyranoski, D., Gilber, N., Ledford, H., Navar, A. and Yahia, M. (2011). Education: the PhD factory. *Nature*, 472(7343), pp.276–9.

Enago Academy (2018). *Thesis Vs. Dissertation*. Available at: https://www.enago.com/academy/thesis-vs-dissertation/ (Accessed: 24 May 2020).

Fapohunda, T.M. (2012). Pay disparity and pay satisfaction in public and private universities in Nigeria. *European Scientific Journal*, 8(28), pp.120–33.

Gbenu, J.P. (2013). Academic staff turnover, national development and emerging policy issues. *Scholars Journal of Arts, Humanities and Social Sciences*, 1(1), pp.1–7.

Golding, C., Sharmini, S. and Lazarovitch, A. (2014). What examiners do: what thesis students should know. *Assessment & Evaluation in Higher Education*, 39(5), pp.563–76, DOI: 10.1080/02602938.2013.859230.

Green, B.N. and Johnson, C.D. (2006). How to write a case report for publication. *Journal of Chiropractic Medicine*, 5(2), pp.77–82.

Guccione, K. and Wellington, J. (2017). *Taking Control of Writing Your Thesis*. London: Bloomsbury.

Hackman, J.R. and Oldham, G.R. (1976). Motivation through the design of work: test of a theory. *Organizational Behavior and Human Performance*, 16, pp.250–79.

Hackman, J.R. and Oldham, G.R. (1980). *Work Redesign*. Reading, MA: Addison-Wesley.

Haidar, H. (2020). What is a PhD? *Top Universities*, 24 January [Online]. Available at: https://www.topuniversities.com/blog/what-phd (Accessed: 11 June 2020).

Harper, D. (2015). Special interest research groups. *Researchers Quarterly*, 3(2), p.9.

Hemingway, E. (n.d.). Ernest Hemingway quotes, *BrainyQuote.com*. Available at: https://www.brainyquote.com/quotes/ernest_hemingway_152929 (Accessed: 11 June 2020).

Herzberg, F. (1987). *One More Time: How Do You Motivate Employees?* Boston, MA: Harvard Business Review.

Herzberg, F., Mausner, B. and Snyderman, B.B. (1959). *The Motivation to Work*. New York: Wiley.

Inekwe, J.N. (2015). The contribution of R&D expenditure to economic growth in developing economies. *Social Indicators Research*, 124(3), pp.727–45.

Iornem, D. (2014). *Teacher Motivation and Job Satisfaction in Nigeria: A Case Study and Guide to Principals, School Proprietors and Education Administrators*. Kaduna: JVC Press.

Iornem, K.S. (2017). A Comparative Analysis of Job Satisfaction and Turnover Intentions Among Lecturers in Public and Privately-Owned Universities in Nigeria. PhD thesis. Cardiff Metropolitan University. Available at: https://repository.cardiffmet.ac.uk/handle/10369/9184 (Accessed: 18 September 2020).

Iornem, K.S. (2018). A Comparative analysis of job satisfaction and turnover intentions among university lecturers in Nigeria. *Journal of Higher Education Theory and Practice*, 18(7). Available at: https://doi.org/10.33423/jhetp.v18i7.264 (Accessed: 19 September).

Iornem, K.S. (2020a). *Job Satisfaction and Turnover Intentions Among University Lecturers in Nigeria*. Kaduna: JVC Press.

Iornem, K.S. (2020b). *International Students' Perspectives on Surviving a PhD in the United Kingdom: Navigating the Emotional and Academic Journey*. Unpublished.

Jones, L. and Loftus, P. (2009). *Time Well Spent: Getting Things Done Through Effective Time Management*. London: Kogan Page Limited.

Kidder, L.H. and Judd, C.M. (1986). *Research Methods in Social Relations*, 5th edn. Japan: CBS Publishing Ltd.

Koenigsberger, J. (2015). Email to Kohol Iornem, 24 November.

Lawson, T.J. and Smith, R.A. (1996). Formatting APA pages in WordPerfect: an update. *Teaching of Psychology*, 23(1), pp.56–8.

Li, M., Liu, X. and Zhang, L. (2015). Health sciences journals: an overview of outputs by Chinese authors. *Health Information and Libraries Journal*, 32(4), pp.255–64.

Loughborough University, (n.d.). *Research* [Online]. Available at: https://www.lboro.ac.uk/departments/sbe/research/interest-groups/ (Accessed: 11 June 2020).

Lowe, M. (n.d.). Plagiarism: what it is and how to avoid it [PowerPoint file]. Available at: www.ulm.edu/~lowe/plagiarism.ppt (Accessed: 11 June 2020).

Lukins, S. (2018). *6 Ways You Can Fund Your PhD* [Online]. Available at: https://www.topuniversities.com/student-info/scholarship-advice/6-ways-you-can-fund-your-phd (Accessed: 11 June 2020).

Marten, S. (2015). The Challenges Facing Academic Staff in UK Universities. *jobs.ac.uk* [Online]. Available at: https://career-advice.jobs.ac.uk/academic/the-challenges-facing-academic-staff-in-uk-universities/ (Accessed: 11 June 2020).

McCann, K. (2016). This is what the ballot paper for the EU referendum vote will look like, *The Telegraph*, 26 January [Online]. Available at: https://www.telegraph.co.uk/news/newstopics/eureferendum/12122349/This-is-what-the-ballot-paper-for-the-EU-referendum-vote-will-look-like.html (Accessed: 11 June 2020).

Might, M. (2010). *The Illustrated Guide to a Ph.D.* Available at: http://matt.might.net/articles/phd-school-in-pictures/ (Accessed: 11 June 2020).

Mobley, W.H. (1977). Intermediate linkages in the relationship between job satisfaction and employee turnover. *Journal of Applied Psychology*, 62(2), pp.237–40.

Ogunleye, A. O. (2000). *An Introduction to Research Methods in Education and Social Sciences.* Lagos: Sunshine International Publications Ltd.

Ologunde, A.O., Akindele, R.I. and Akande, W.O. (2013). Moonlighting among university lecturers and their performance in the south-western Nigeria. *Journal of Management and Sustainability*, 3(4), pp.92–102.

Ologunde, A.O., Asaolu, T.O. and Elumilade, D.O. (2007). Labour turnover among university teachers in southwestern Nigeria – issues, solutions and lessons. *African Journal of Public Administration and Management*, 18(2), 72–85.

Oshagbemi, T. (1999). Academics and their managers: a comparative study in job satisfaction. *Personnel Review*, 28(1–2), pp.108–23. Available at: https://doi.org/10.1108/00483489910249027 (Accessed: 7 August 2020).

Oshagbemi, T. and Hickson, C. (2003). Some aspects of overall job satisfaction: a binomial logit model. *Journal of Managerial Psychology*, 18(4), pp.357–67.

Pappas, C. (2013). *Top 10 Free Plagiarism Detection Tools For eLearning Professionals* (2020 Update) [Online]. Available at: https://elearningindustry.com/top-10-free-plagiarism-detection-tools-for-teachers (Accessed: 11 June 2020).

Patel, N. (2015). Writing up your thesis: summary of thesis completion workshop, 26 October 2015. *Researchers Quarterly*, 3(3), p.8.

Postgrad.com (n.d.). *Doing a PhD: Why it's Important to Publish* [Online]. Available at: https://www.postgrad.com/advice/phd/why_its_important_to_publish/ (Accessed: 11 June 2020).

ProjectManager (n.d.). *The Ultimate Guide to: Gantt Charts.* Available at: https://www.projectmanager.com/gantt-chart (Accessed: 11 June 2020).

Rist, D. (2016). *Neuro Linguistic Coaching for Personal Performance*, 3rd edn. Kent: The Academy of Neuro Linguistic Coaching.

Ruttan, V.W. (1998). The new growth theory and development economics: a survey. *The Journal of Development Studies*, 35(2), pp.1–26, DOI: 10.1080/00220389808422562.

Saeidi, M. (2016). Comment on: Mohamad, S.N.A., How to write a good thesis abstract? What are the components should have in writing a clear and good abstract?, *Research Gate* [Online]. Comment posted 2016. Available at: https://www.researchgate.net/post/How_to_write_a_good_thesis_abstract (Accessed: 11 June 2020).

Satope, B.F. and Akintunde, T.S. (2013). Factors of labour mobility in Nigerian universities. *IOSR Journal of Humanities and Social Science*, 11(1), pp.28–33.

Sauermann, H. and Roach, M. (2016). Why pursue the postdoc path? *Science*, 352(6286), pp.663–4.

Shahedi, B. (2015). Comment on: White, J.S., What is the average length of a doctoral thesis? *Research Gate* [Online]. Comment posted 2015. Available at: https://www.researchgate.net/post/What_is_the_average_length_of_a_doctoral_thesis (Accessed: 25 May 2020).

Shannon, B. (2017). Success is where preparation and opportunity meet, *The Irish News*, 18 July. Available at: https://www.irishnews.com/business/2017/07/18/news/success-is-where-preparation-and-opportunity-meet-1086316/ (Accessed: 25 May 2020).

Shaw, H.J. (2017). Email to Kohol Iornem, 23 May.

Ssesanga, K. and Garrett, R.M. (2005). Job satisfaction of university academics: perspectives from Uganda. *Higher Education*, 50(1), pp.33–56.

Szomszor, M., Pendlebury, D.A. and Adams, J. (2020). How much is too much? The difference between research influence and self-citation excess. *Scientometrics*, 123, pp.1119–47. Available at: https://doi.org/10.1007/s11192-020-03417-5 (Accessed: 7 August 2020).

Taylor, H. (2018). *Your Most Important Time Management Tool.* Available at: https://www.taylorintime.com/your-most-important-time-management-tool/ (Accessed: 25 May 2020).

The Hillingdon Hospital (2006). *Sample in Research.* Available at: https://www.thh.nhs.uk/documents/_Departments/Research/InfoSheets/16_sampling_research.pdf (Accessed: 25 May 2020).

Thomson, P. (2014). Connecting chapters/chapter introductions, *patter* [Online]. Available at: https://patthomson.net/2014/01/16/connecting-chapterschapter-introductions/ (Accessed: 11 June 2020).

Tracy, B. (2017). *Eat that Frog! 21 Great Ways to Stop Procrastinating and Get More Done in Less Time,* 3rd edn. Oakland, CA: Berrett-Koehler Publishers.

Turla, P. (2006). *Time Management Tips: How to Set Priorities and Improve Your Time Management Skills* [Online video] 29 October. Available at: https://www.youtube.com/watch?v=1rFMWRYnT18 (Accessed: 11 June 2020).

Turnitin.com (n.d.). *Education with Integrity.* Available at: https://www.turnitin.com/ (Accessed: 9 June 2020).

UCL Institute of Education (2018). *Scholarly Communication: Finding Impact Factors for Journals* [Online]. Available at: https://libguides.ioe.ac.uk/c.php?g=482311&p=3299102 (Accessed: 11 June 2020).

Umaru, R.I. and Ombugus, D.A. (2017). Determinants of job satisfaction of colleges of education lecturers: a study of Nasarawa State College of Education, Akwanga. *International Journal of Humanities Social Sciences and Education (IJHSSE),* 4, pp.1–7.

University College London, (n.d.). *Guidance on How to Contact Potential Supervisors* [Online]. Available at: https://www.ucl.ac.uk/prospective-students/graduate/sites/prospective-students_graduate/files/potential-supervisor.pdf (Accessed: 11 June 2020).

University of Cambridge (n.d.). *Word Limits and Requirements of your Degree Committee.* Available at: https://www.cambridgestudents.cam.ac.uk/your-course/examinations/graduate-exam-information/submitting-and-examination/phd-msc-mlitt/word (Accessed: 11 June 2020).

University of Exeter Business School (2014). *A Guide to Citing, Referencing and Avoiding Plagiarism.* Available at: https://ask.fxplus.ac.uk/sites/default/files/public/page/200-Business%20School%20-%20APA%20Referencing/attached/UEBS_2014_A_Guide_to_Citing%2C_Referencing_and_Avoiding_Plagiarism_V.2.0_2014.pdf (Accessed: 25 May 2020).

University of Glasgow (n.d.). *Shared Interest Groups* [Online]. Available at: https://www.gla.ac.uk/researchinstitutes/bahcm/research/sigs/ (Accessed: 6 August 2020).

University of Leeds (n.d.). *Leeds Harvard Referencing Examples* [Online]. Available at: https://library.leeds.ac.uk/referencing-examples/9/leeds-harvard (Accessed: 25 May 2020).

University of Leicester (2011). *Management Research Degrees* [Leaflet obtained in School of Management], 15 August.

University of Leicester (n.d. a). *Practice Viva Questions* [Online]. Available at: https://www2.le.ac.uk/departments/doctoralcollege/training/eresources/study-guides/viva/prepare/questions (Accessed: 11 June 2020).

University of Leicester (n.d. b). *Formatting Your Thesis and Word Limits.* Available at: https://www2.le.ac.uk/departments/doctoralcollege/training/eresources/study-guides/thesis/format-guidelines/format-guidelines (Accessed: 6 August 2020).

Yorke, H. (2018). New university plagiarism software to be launched in crackdown on 'contract' cheating, *The Telegraph,* 1 February. Available at: https://www.telegraph.co.uk/education/2018/02/01/new-university-plagiarism-software-launched-crackdown-contract/ (Accessed: 11 June 2020).

Index

3S approach (story, structure, sentences) 49

abstracts 51–2
amendments 68–9
AMR *see* annual monitoring report
annual monitoring report (AMR) 20–1
application and entry requirements 17
   competency in English language 17
   master's degree 17
   proposal and personal statement 17

British Academy of Management 53

Cardiff Metropolitan University 32–3
career options (academia vs other employment) 55–7
communication 41–2
concerns, fears and reservations 12–14
copying 33–4
corrections 67–8
CVs 19, 21, 70

data analysis and recording systems 4, 5–6, 7
   collecting 30
   examiner expectations 74
   integrity of 30–1
   planning 29–30
dissertation 23

editor 63–5
external examiner 70–1
   difficult 77–8
   reading the work 71–3
   what they are looking for 73
      citations 76
      clarity and rationale 74
      contributions to knowledge 74
      data analysis 74
      focus and recommendation 74
      formatting 74
      grammatical and typographical errors 73
      referencing 74–5
      understanding the topic 73
      verification of introduction and summary 73

fieldwork 30
funding 15, 17
   charities 16
   crowdfunding 16
   employer sponsorship 16
   postgraduate loan 16
   research council grant 16
   studentship 16

IELTS *see* International English Language Testing System
International English Language Testing System (IELTS) 17
interview 20, 85–6

Journal of Higher Education Theory and Practice 53–4

key result area (KRA) 40–1
KISS (keep it short and simple) 45
KRA *see* key result area

language competency 17
legal realities 3, 4, 10–11
literature review 24–5, 29
literature sources 95–100

meetings 42
   online 82
mental and emotional preparedness 7
milestones 14
mock viva 21
   definition 66
   online 82
   successful
      don'ts 81–2
      dos 78–81
motivation 4, 6–7, 8, 12–13, 58–9

motivators
  colleagues 60–1
  family 61
  father 60
  PhD friends at other universities 61
  professional capacity 62
  proofreader 60
  supervisory team 59–60
MPhil degree 20, 21
multitasking 39–40

online viva and meetings 82
  application familiarization 82
  internet connection 82
  PC complies with app 82
  personal appearance and quiet
    environment 82
originality 24–6

Pareto 80/0 rule 40
perfectionism 67–8
PhD
  definition 23
  journey
    advice 9–10
    background 1–2
    conclusions and recommendations
      10–11
    hindsight 10
    initial fears and concerns 9
    international experiences 3–8
    questions concerning 2
    reasons for embarking
      on 8–9
    toughest part of 9
  originality 24–6
  research
    extensive 26–8
    original 24
    planning 29–31
  thesis or dissertation 23
  upgrade from MPhil 20
plagiarisers 43
plagiarism 32
  avoiding 35–6
  definitions 32–3
  detecting and reporting 36
  software checkers 36–7
  types
    copying 33–4
    paraphrasing 34–5

    patchwork 34
    unintentional 35
planning
  prime needs and responsibilities
    13–14
  research 29–31
PowerPoint presentation 44–6
procrastination 42
progress agenda 14
proofreader
  finding 63–5
  as motivator 60
publication 53–4
  adapting to requirements 55
  importance 54

references
  consistency 37
  examiner expectations 74–5
  styles 38
research
  access to 5
  areas of 11
  dealing with changes 66–9
  extensive 26–8
  methods and methodology 3, 4, 28
  originality
    critical literature review 24–5
    further research method 25
    observation or problem statement
      method 25–6
    replication 25
  planning
    data analysis 31
    data integrity 30–1
    data-collection 29–30
    focus 29
    literature review 29
    participants 30
    question formulation 29
    resources required 31
  proposal (writing and organizing)
    17–18
  reliability and validity 28
  skills 32
    consistency in referencing 37–8
    join research interest group 43–4
    plagiarism 32–7
    PowerPoint presentation 44–6
    time management 38–43
viva questions 90

Research Interest Group (RIG)
    aim 43
    benefits 43–4
    definition 43
RIG *see* Research Interest Group

supervisors
    availability and contacting 4, 5, 19–20
    in-house vs contractual 6
    relationship 3, 4–5, 8, 9, 59–60
    reputation 66–7
    responding to feedback 66
system failures 41
systematic study 27–8

Test of English as a Foreign Language
    (TOEFL) 17
thesis 23
    abstract 51–2
    argumentation
        3S approach 49
        questioning articles 49
        tips 50
    examiner expectations 73–6
    making it easy to read 71
        conclusion and summary 72
        introduction 71–2
        table of contents 72–3
    structure 47–8
    summarizing 86, 93–4
    word count 47, 48
time management 38
    distraction and interruptions 40–1
    meetings 42
    multitasking 39–40
    personal disorganization 38–9
    poor communication 41–2

procrastination 42
    system failure 41
TOEFL *see* Test of English as a Foreign
    Language

UCL *see* University College London
UK Visas and Immigration (UKVI) 10–11
UKVI *see* UK Visas and Immigration
University College London (UCL) 19
University of Glasgow 43–4

viva voce 21–2
    personal experience 84–9
        asked to make corrections 88
        awareness of post-thesis
            research 87
        buying time 88
        explanation of theories and data
            analysis 87
        interview format 85–6
        maintaining eye contact 88–9
        questions and answers 86
        summary of thesis 86
    possible outcomes 84
    sample questions 89
        analysis and findings 91
        conclusions and implications 91
        discussion 91
        general 89–90
        research context 90
        research methods 90
    successful
        don'ts 81–2
        dos 78–81

work–life balance 3, 4–5, 10

Printed in Great Britain
by Amazon